CW00590508

Collins

YOU CAN PAINT

Seashore in Watercolour

JUNE CRAWSHAW paints in watercolour, acrylic and oil. She is a member of the Society of Women Artists, the British Watercolour Society, the National Acrylic Painters Association and is an Honorary member of the United Society of Artists. In 1992 she helped found and launch the Society of Amateur Artists. June writes articles for *Leisure Painter* magazine and has featured in three television series with her husband Alwyn, which have been screened by Channel 4 worldwide. She has her work published as fine art prints and greetings cards, and teaches watercolour painting in the UK and abroad.

Collins

YOU CAN PAINT

Seashore in Watercolour

A step-by-step guide for
ABSOLUTE BEGINNERS

JUNE CRAWSHAW

First published in 2004 by
Collins, an imprint of
HarperCollins*Publishers*
77-85 Fulham Palace Road
Hammersmith
London W6 8JB

Collins is a registered trademark of
HarperCollins Publishers Limited

The Collins website address is
www.collins.co.uk

05 07 09 08 06 04
2 4 6 8 7 5 3 1

A catalogue record of this book is available from the British Library

Editor: Isobel Smales
Designer: Penny Dawes
Photographer: Nigel Cheffers-Heard

ISBN 0 00 714383 4

Colour reproduction by Colourscan, Singapore
Printed and bound in Italy by L.E.G.O

Contents

INTRODUCTION

The seashore can be both an exciting and a very relaxing subject to paint. I was lucky enough to live near the sea for nine years, and I painted many pictures of the seashore, seeing it in all its fabulous moods. In the summer, it is crowded with holidaymakers. If your family and friends are not painters, being by the sea gives you a wonderful opportunity to sketch while they swim or sunbathe. You can paint anything from a single pebble or shell to the pier, the cliffs, or a beach busy with people.

In the winter, when it's empty of people, the seashore is just as stimulating. It can be alive with seabirds, another great subject for painting. Or the sea can be rough, with gathering clouds overhead, which is very exciting. If it is too wet and windy you may not be able to sit and paint, but you can still take photographs, and using these and your memories you can paint wonderfully atmospheric paintings when you

Playing Together
25 x 38 cm (10 x 15 in)
Bockingford
watercolour paper

Corbiere Lighthouse, Jersey *28 x 38 cm (11 x 15 in)*
Bockingford watercolour paper

return home. Any time of the day or year, the seashore has unlimited subjects to paint.

This book means exactly what its title says. If you follow my exercises and practise them until you are happy with the results, you *can* paint the seashore. By the time you get to the end of the book, you will be familiar with the subject and will enjoy painting it. You may not yet be producing masterpieces, but you will be on the road to success. Remember, the more you practise, the better you will get. Some people learn quickly, others take more time. You are not in a race; take your own time.

Every artist has his or her own style of painting. This usually develops once you have gained experience. Let this happen naturally; it is your personality shining through in your painting, and people will soon recognize it.

Once you have mastered this book, take your sketchbook with you whenever you go to the seashore. You may feel shy at first, I know I did, but your confidence will grow with every outdoor sketch you do.

June Crawshaw

How to use this book

If you are like me, you will look through this book and get very excited and want to start painting straight away. Don't! Read the book thoroughly before you attempt to put paint on paper. You will then be more familiar with the subject and the way I teach. Then you can get your brushes out and start.

If you are a beginner and are unsure which materials to get, I begin by listing the basic ones you will need (pages 10–11). These are the materials I have used throughout the book.

The first lesson is colour mixing, because I believe it is the most important technique to master. Without a good knowledge of it you will find painting is most frustrating. You don't need to have a scientific knowledge of colour mixing, it simply means that you should get plenty of practice mixing your colours and experimenting. I go on to show you how to master certain watercolour techniques. These demonstrate different ways you can apply paint to paper, or even take it off. Once you have mastered these, many of your painting questions will have been answered.

Bathers on the Beach
17.5 x 22.5 cm (7 x 9 in) Bockingford watercolour paper

Sun and Wind at Dawlish *38 x 30 cm (15 x 12 in)*
Bockingford watercolour paper

The book is full of exercises for you to practise. Remember, practice is all important. If some of your work is less than perfect, don't worry; the more you do the sooner you will improve. Don't try to make every brush stroke exactly the same as mine; you will be too anxious and will not be able to let the paint flow. Go for the overall look and enjoy painting it. Also, don't stay on one technique or exercise too long; if you can't do it, try again later as the chances are you will find it much easier, and make a success of it.

I have also included some sketches for you to copy. These show you that when you are out sketching your work is often much simpler because of weather conditions, comfort and time constraints and you can't put in the same detail as you would indoors.

There are three demonstrations which are all photographed at different stages of completion. This allows you to actually see the painting as it progresses through to the finished work, and enables you to follow the whole painting process from the beginning to the end. I have kept the instructions for all the exercises and demonstrations easy to follow, to help you to progress smoothly through the book.

BASIC MATERIALS

The wonderful thing about watercolour is that you don't need a complicated range of materials to begin with. A pad or some watercolour paper, a couple of brushes and a few paints will enable you to paint wonderful pictures. Once you have got over the hurdle of learning the essentials, you may want to experiment with different papers, brushes and paints, but keep it simple to start with, and work with the materials listed here, which I have used throughout this book.

Colours I only use seven colours, which I recommend for all the exercises in this book: two reds (Alizarin Crimson and Cadmium Red), two yellows (Yellow Ochre and Cadmium Yellow Pale), two blues (French Ultramarine and Coeruleum), and one ready-mixed green (Hooker's Green Dark) (see pages 12–13). There are two qualities of paint, Artists' and Students'. Although I use Artists' quality, Daler-Rowney Students' Georgian are very good and less expensive.

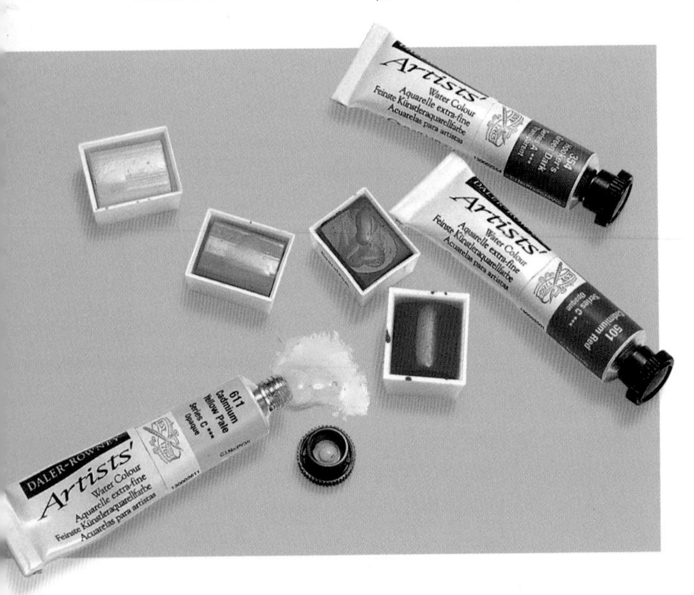

Brushes Your brushes are very important; they become part of you when you paint. It is essential to experiment with them and really get to know them. I use two sable brushes, a No.10 as my large brush and a No.6 as my small brush (the higher the number, the larger the brush). Sable brushes are more expensive than synthetic brushes, but they hold more water, which is important in watercolour painting. I also use a synthetic brush, a Dalon series D99 No. 2 rigger; I prefer this to a sable rigger brush, which I find too soft. You can use all synthetic brushes if you prefer.

Paper There are many different papers available. Here I have used Bockingford watercolour paper and cartridge drawing paper. Both are inexpensive and they are my favourite papers. One of the golden rules for watercolour painting is always to have your paper at an angle to allow the paint to run

I use pans of colour rather than tubes, as I can control the amount on the brush more easily

These are the materials you will need for the exercises in the book

slowly down the paper. If you feel rather frightened confronting a blank piece of paper, don't worry: many people feel the same way, and even the first few pencil lines you draw will break the spell.

Other equipment I use a 2B pencil for drawing: it is quite soft so it is good for fine and heavy lines and shading. I also use a putty eraser, as it doesn't damage the paper if used gently. A Stanley knife or penknife is essential for sharpening your pencil. Kitchen paper and tissues will come in useful, and finally you will need a water container such as a jam jar. If practicable you may like to have a portable seat. Now you are ready to paint!

EASY COLOUR MIXING

You can mix almost any colour from the three primary colours: red, yellow and blue. There are different shades of red, yellow and blue, so you can make many variations by mixing different primary colours together. Always keep your colours in the same place in your paintbox, as colour mixing is much easier if you know where each colour is.

Starter palette

I suggest you start with the colours I use: Alizarin Crimson, Yellow Ochre, French Ultramarine, Cadmium Red, Coeruleum, Cadmium Yellow Pale and Hooker's Green Dark. Using a ready-mixed green with other colours makes a wide range of greens quickly, which is especially useful when painting outdoors.

I use the three colours on the opposite page for most of a painting, and you can paint a whole picture using just these three colours. But the four colours shown below help to give more variety in your colour mixes. They are also used for 'local' colours, for example, Cadmium Red for a bright red fishing boat or Coeruleum for a bright blue swimming costume.

Cadmium Red

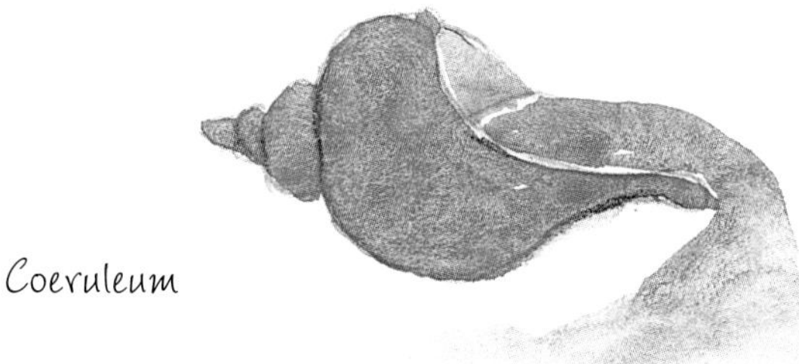

Coeruleum

If you want to show sunlit sand you would use Cadmium Yellow Pale because this is a much brighter shade than Yellow Ochre. Hooker's Green Dark is a very bright green, so it is best used in very small amounts mixed with other colours, or on its own with plenty of water.

Cadmium Yellow Pale

Hooker's Green Dark

Mixing two colours

When mixing colours, always put the predominant colour with water first. If you are mixing a yellowish-orange the yellow would go in first because it is the predominant colour, then you add a little red until you have a yellowish-orange. When painting with watercolour, you add more water to make your colours paler.

The colour on the left of each shell is the predominant colour with a smaller amount of the second colour (seen on the right side of the shell) added. When the two mix they make the colour shown coming out of the shell. More water is added to make the mixed colour paler.

Mixing three colours

Below I have mixed some seashore colours using only three colours from the palette. The larger blob of colour shows the predominant colour, and you add smaller amounts of the other colours except when you are mixing the sea colours where the original colours are of equal importance. Use these colour mixes as a general guide.

Basic techniques

Now you can start to put paint onto paper to see what happens. The next few pages show you some exciting techniques that will help you become a fully fledged seashore artist. You will get to know your brushes and paints and the effects you can achieve with them, beginning by trying wet-on-wet, then learning to control the paint by practising washes.

Wet-on-wet

Just look at all this colour! I know you can't wait to start. Mix plenty of different colours in your palette, fill your brush with wet paint, put it onto the paper and just see what happens. Then dip your brush into another colour and run it into the first (use plenty of water). Keep doing this, play around and look at the effects.

Basic washes

The wash is a very important technique in watercolour painting. You need to mix plenty of water with your paint and remember that your paper needs to be at an angle so that the paint can run slowly down the paper and the brush strokes merge together.

Flat wash *Fill your large brush with watery paint and, starting at the top of the paper, take the brush stroke right across the paper and lift it off. Fill your brush again and do another stroke underneath, running it into the bottom of the first wet stroke. Continue until the area is covered.*

Graded wash *This wash is good for skies, when you want the colour to get gradually paler. Work the same way as you did for the flat wash, but instead of using the same colour add water into the colour mix as you go down the paper until it is nearly all water.*

Graded colour wash

This is another good wash for skies, especially sunsets. You paint this wash the same way as the flat wash, this time changing colour as you go.

Start with blue, add red on the way down, and then yellow. Remember to use plenty of water in your paint.

Wet-on-dry

To get a hard edge you must let the underneath paint dry. You can then paint on top of it and the wet paint won't merge into the dry paint underneath.

Directional wash

This is still a wash but your brush strokes go in different directions. This wash can be painted large or small and, unlike a flat wash, it is not restricted to a uniform shape.

Keep the brush full of watery paint and don't let the paint on the paper dry. If you keep it wet you can paint around any shapes and the paint strokes will merge together.

Brushmarks

Different sized brushes make different marks. The marks also vary depending on how much paint and water you have in the brush and how hard you press it down on the paper. Experiment to discover the different effects you can achieve. I have used my small brush for these exercises.

The top stroke is made with the point of the brush. The middle one is made by pressing the brush down harder on the paper. For the bottom stroke, use the side of the brush and press down hard; this brush stroke only creates a straight top edge, which can then be filled in underneath.

For the curved stroke start lightly, then press down, and finish lightly. For the stroke far right, press down and work from the top, then turn the brush half over on its thin edge and continue down in one stroke.

Press down on the hairs at the ferrule end (nearest the handle) and move the brush from side to side on the paper. This gives you broken edges, good for subjects such as clouds, a rough beach, breaking waves and bushes.

Dry brush

How can you paint with a dry brush? Well, it isn't actually dry, just dryer than normal, so if you drag the brush along the paper the paint hits and misses as it goes along, leaving some white paper showing. This gives a lovely sparkly effect which is very good for painting water or pebbles on the beach. This technique is more effective on rough-surfaced paper.

Here, the dry-brush technique is used to show sunlight sparkling on the sea.

A few darker marks over dry-brush 'sand' give the impression of pebbles on a beach.

Using a rigger brush

The hairs on a rigger brush are long and thin and all the same length. This enables a brush full of wet paint to continue producing the same thickness of line for a long time. The less pressure you use the thinner the line is. A rigger is mainly used for painting the rigging on boats, but is useful wherever you need to paint fine lines.

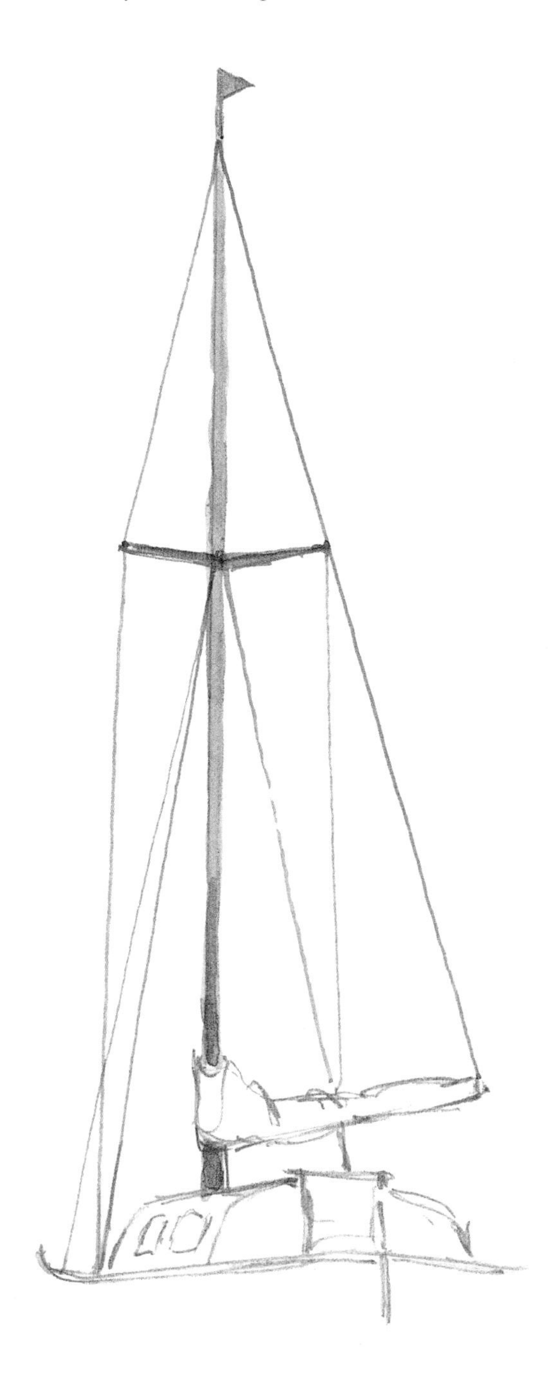

You can use a rigger for fences, grasses, twigs on trees, and you can also draw with it. It is very versatile; a fabulous brush. I wouldn't be without one. Practise these brush strokes and experiment for yourself.

Lifting out with a brush

Lifting out removes areas of paint from your picture. Generally with watercolour you leave white paper showing if you want light-coloured areas. But sometimes you will want to paint the background in one wash, or you think your painting looks dull and needs something more in it to give it life. This is when you could try lifting out. Not all papers are suitable for lifting out. The paper I used for this exercise is Bockingford watercolour paper, which is excellent.

Get a tissue, clean water and a clean brush. Make sure the original paint is dry, then take your brush with clean water in it and brush the shape you want to lift out, over and over again, then blot it with the tissue. You may have to do this more than once.

Blotting out with a tissue

Blotting out is another technique used to remove paint from your picture, but unlike lifting out, where the original paint has to be dry, when you use the blotting-out technique the paint must be wet. A rolled-up tissue is used to remove areas of wet paint. Blotting out is more spontaneous than lifting out, which makes it a more suitable technique for soft subjects with irregular outlines such as the clouds and waves shown below.

Paint in the blue sky, leaving some paper white. Screw up a tissue and while the sky is still wet blot out cloud shapes. When dry, paint in the cloud shadows.

Add a little green to blue and paint in the sea, leaving some white unpainted paper. While this is still wet, blot out the spray on the waves with a tissue, then paint in the sand. Simple, but effective.

Shadows

Shadows are very important in a painting, as they add sunshine and life. To paint shadows successfully, all you have to know is how to mix the shadow colour and where the light is coming from. Shadows vary in length depending on the time of day, and are darker or lighter depending on the strength of the light. Shadows also help to make objects look three dimensional (see page 25).

Because watercolour is transparent, when you paint the shadow colour the underneath colour will show through, but darker, giving the illusion of a shadow.

Here the sun is coming from behind the spade.

The sun is shining from the left of this bucket.

This picture shows a shadow cast by another object, falling on a windbreak.

3-D objects

If you paint a picture without shadows or tone (darker or lighter areas), objects look as flat as the paper. To make any object look three dimensional it must have light or dark areas or patterns on it to show form. Remember that when the light shining on an object is very bright, the shadows are very dark, and they get paler as the light gets softer.

Look at the flat blue disc. By adding tone on the right-hand side it becomes a ball, and the cast shadow from the ball makes it appear to sit on the paper. Rings painted around the ball also create the illusion that it is round.

The two yellow balls are given form in a similar way.

Adding a simple dark shadow to the shape on the left turns it into a three-dimensional bucket and spade.

SHELLS AND PEBBLES

You can always find shells and pebbles on the beach. They have very interesting shapes and wonderful colours. You can paint or draw them where you find them, or take them home to work from. Either way, this is a simple but rewarding subject to practise with your watercolours, and you may also end up with a lovely painting.

Broken shells

This painting has been included to give you inspiration, and to show how just a few varied pebbles and shells can make an interesting painting. Next time you are on the beach, look out for these 'ready-made' subjects.

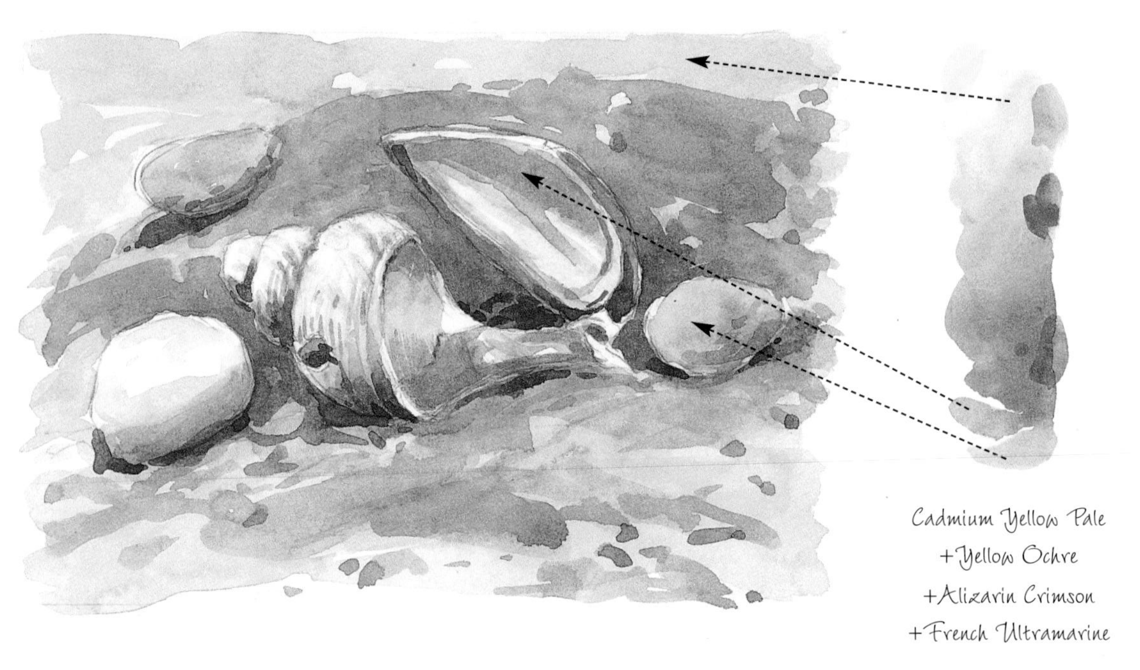

I painted the pale yellow sand wet-on-wet around the pebbles and shells. These were painted next, leaving unpainted paper for highlights. When the background was dry, the dark sand colour was painted to help define the shapes of the shells and pebbles. Finally, I painted in the shadows on the pebbles and shells and their cast shadows on the sand.

Pebbles

When someone says 'paint a pebble' it sounds very uninspiring. But take a closer look at pebbles and you will find beautiful colours and patterns on them. I am always delighted with the pebbles I find on the beach. They are an easy subject for a beginner, because they are such simple shapes.

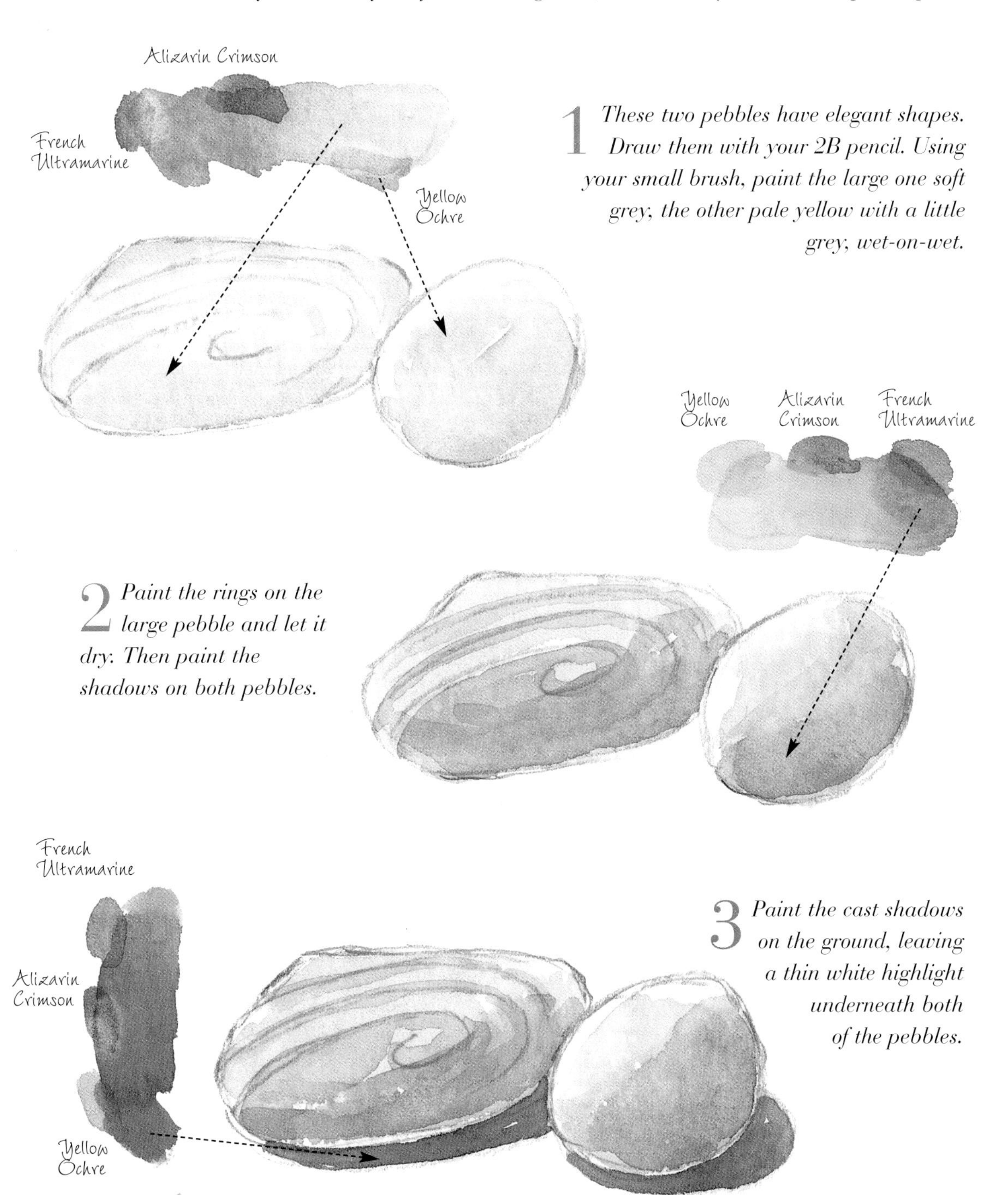

1 *These two pebbles have elegant shapes. Draw them with your 2B pencil. Using your small brush, paint the large one soft grey, the other pale yellow with a little grey, wet-on-wet.*

2 *Paint the rings on the large pebble and let it dry. Then paint the shadows on both pebbles.*

3 *Paint the cast shadows on the ground, leaving a thin white highlight underneath both of the pebbles.*

Scallop shell

This shell is shaped like a fan. Don't worry too much if yours is a little different to mine; concentrate on the ridges and the dark pink lines around the shell as they are important, helping to give it its familiar form.

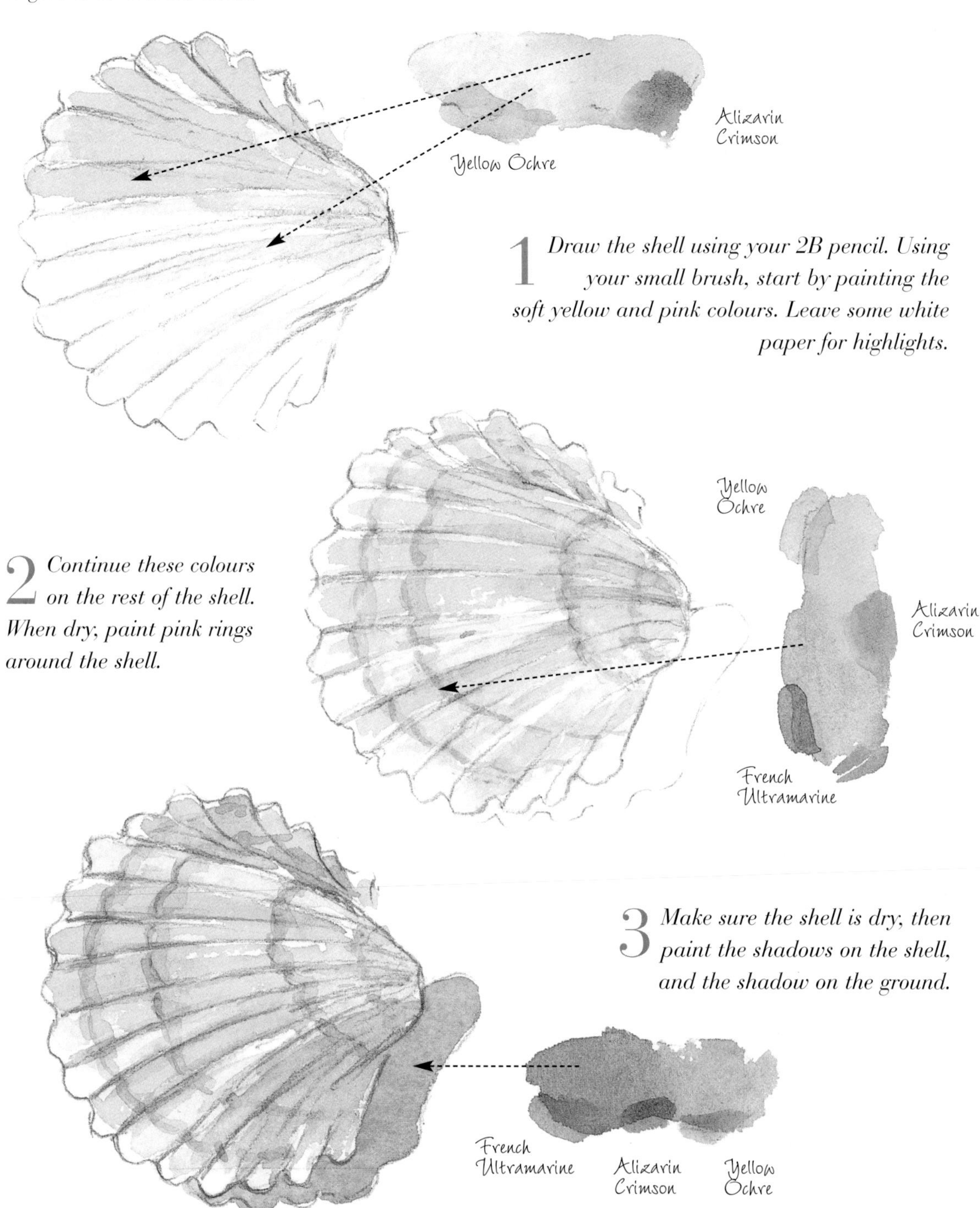

1 *Draw the shell using your 2B pencil. Using your small brush, start by painting the soft yellow and pink colours. Leave some white paper for highlights.*

2 *Continue these colours on the rest of the shell. When dry, paint pink rings around the shell.*

3 *Make sure the shell is dry, then paint the shadows on the shell, and the shadow on the ground.*

Sketching shells

Sketching shells on the beach is almost as easy as painting indoors. The shells don't move, and if you are lucky with the weather you have plenty of time to sketch them. Try copying these sketches. Note how the darks and lights give the shells form and help them to look three dimensional.

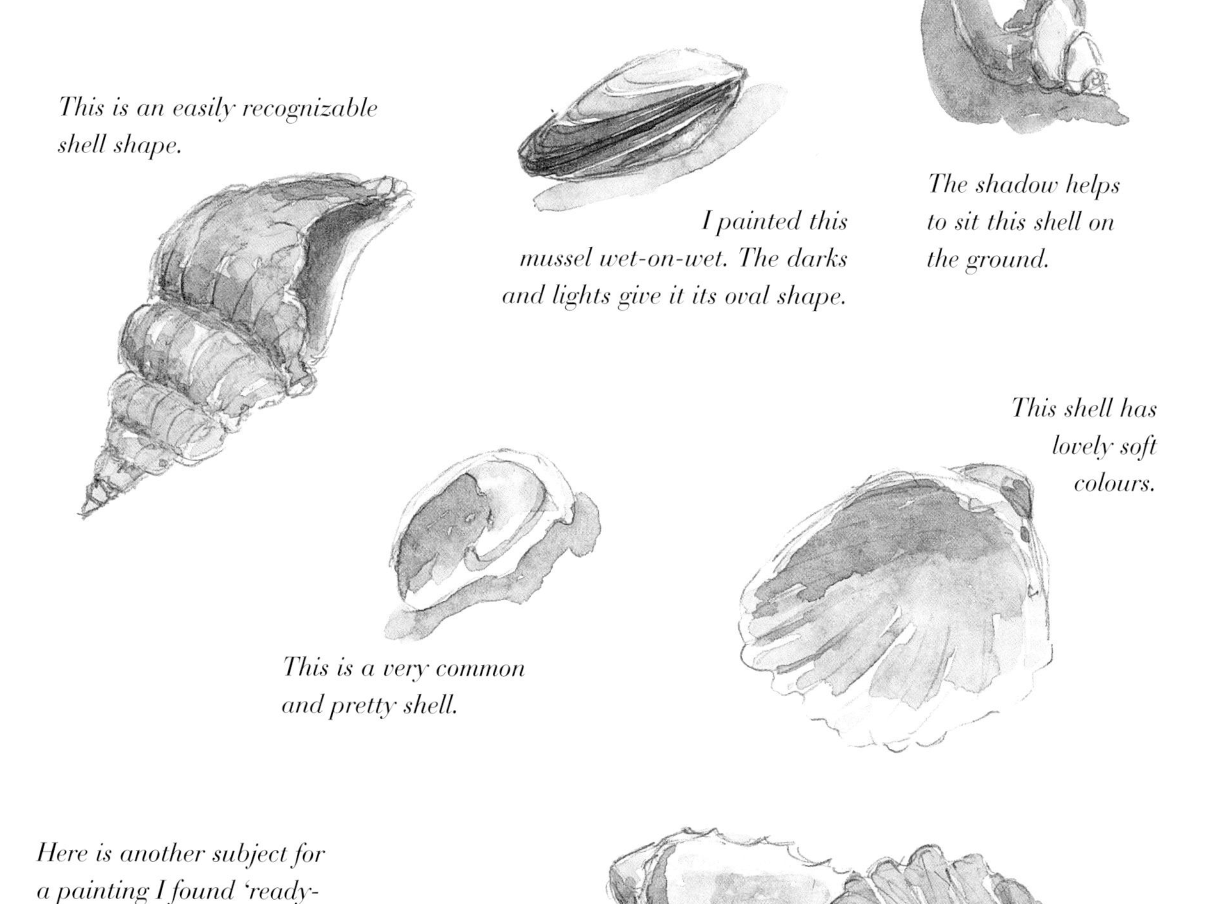

This is an easily recognizable shell shape.

I painted this mussel wet-on-wet. The darks and lights give it its oval shape.

The shadow helps to sit this shell on the ground.

This shell has lovely soft colours.

This is a very common and pretty shell.

Here is another subject for a painting I found 'ready-made' on the beach.

EXERCISE Paint shells and pebbles

By making sure the shells and pebbles aren't too crowded together, you can see their distinct shapes. This makes them easier to paint. The background pebbles are kept less distinct to give the impression that they are in the distance.

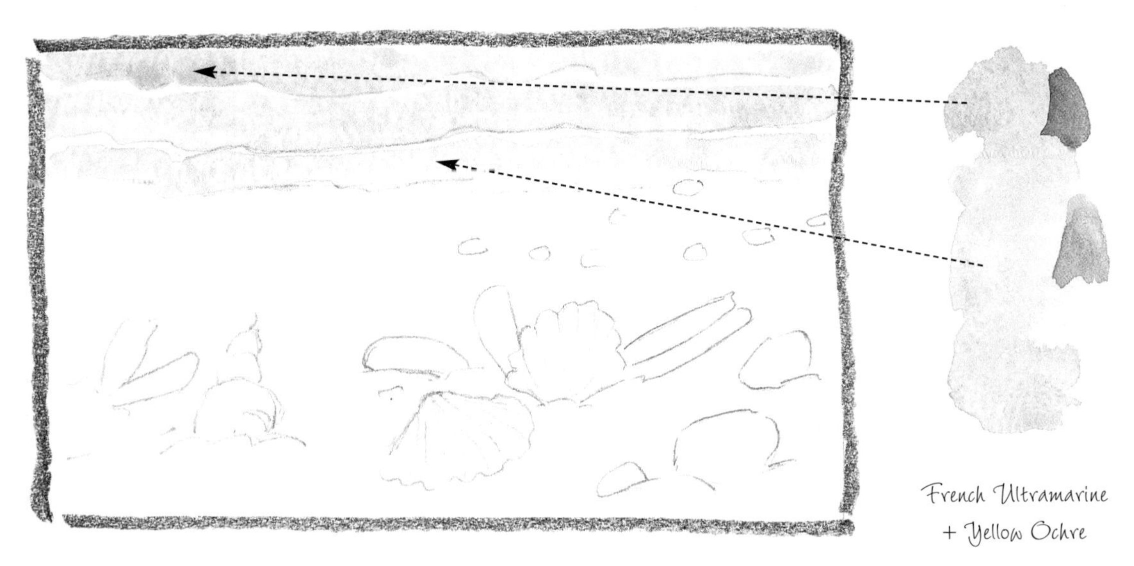

1 *Draw the scene with your 2B pencil, then paint in the sea using your large brush, wet-on-wet.*

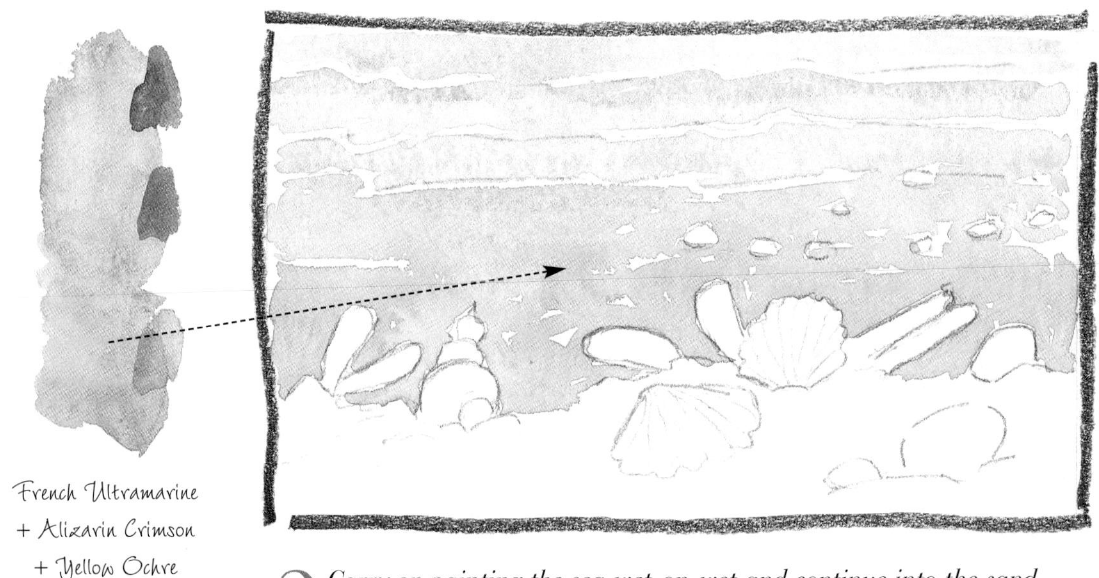

2 *Carry on painting the sea wet-on-wet and continue into the sand around the pebbles and shells.*

The palette

French Ultramarine

Yellow Ochre

Alizarin Crimson

Alizarin Crimson
+ French Ultramarine

3 *When dry, start painting the pebbles and shells with your small brush, leaving some unpainted paper on them for highlights.*

French Ultramarine
+ Alizarin Crimson
+ Yellow Ochre

4 *Paint the foreground sand around the shells and pebbles. Add more colour to these, let them dry, then add shadows.*

MARINE LIFE

Many different living things are found at the seaside. This section illustrates a few of the fascinating fish, seaweeds and crustaceans you may see. After practising painting these, you will be able to paint many others of your own choice. You can also practise painting different types from photographs.

Crabs

Crabs are some of the most commonly seen creatures on the seashore. You will find them in all sorts of environments: in tiny rock pools, under pebbles and in the open sea. They vary greatly in shape, size and colour. Their subtle colouring makes them fascinating for an artist to paint.

I painted the sand around the crabs first with a directional wash. When this was dry, I painted the crabs themselves, varying the colours. Once dry, I painted the shadows on their shells, and on the stones. Finally, I painted the cast shadows on the sand.

Prawn

We are used to seeing pink prawns, but they are this colour only after they have been cooked. The prawns that we see in rock pools are generally similar in colour to the one I have painted here. You will find your rigger brush comes in useful for painting the prawn's long feelers.

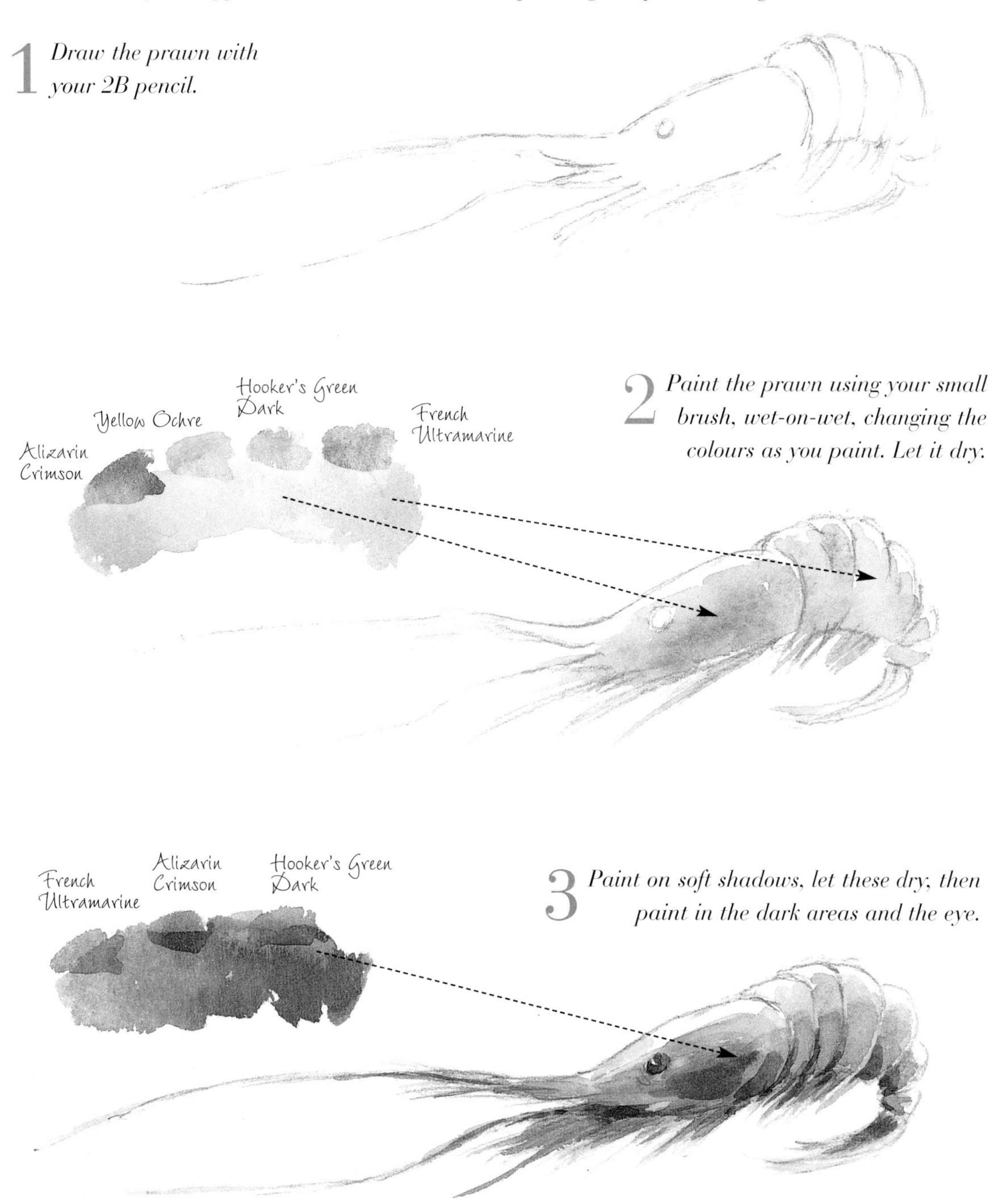

1 *Draw the prawn with your 2B pencil.*

2 *Paint the prawn using your small brush, wet-on-wet, changing the colours as you paint. Let it dry.*

3 *Paint on soft shadows, let these dry, then paint in the dark areas and the eye.*

Starfish

I was walking on my local beach and I was amazed at how many starfish there were. I decided to photograph one in its natural setting and used the photograph to paint from at home. The shape and the colours make an interesting painting.

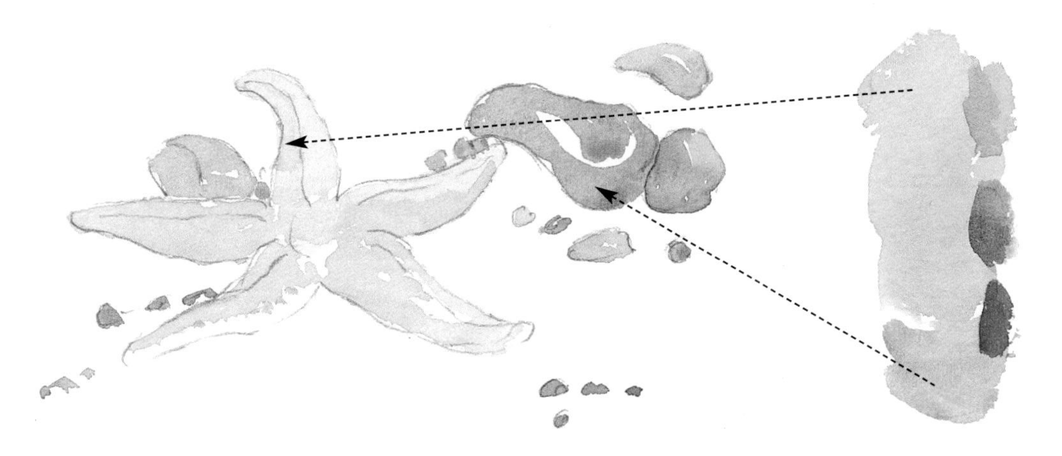

Yellow Ochre
+ Alizarin Crimson
+ French Ultramarine

1 *Draw the starfish and stones with your 2B pencil. Using your small brush, paint the starfish with a pale wash, leaving some white unpainted paper. Paint the grey stones, leaving highlights on the large one. Now paint the orange stones and leave to dry.*

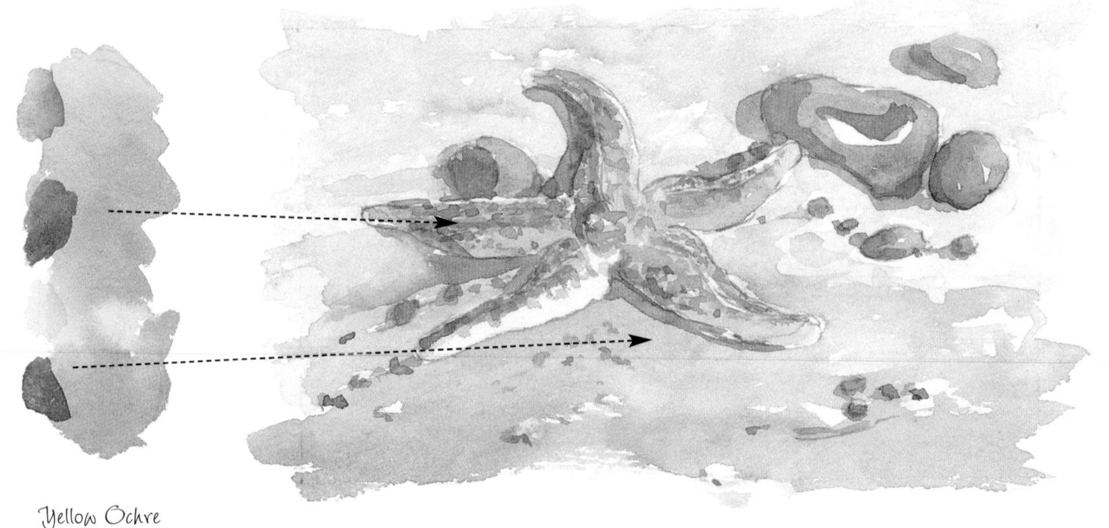

Yellow Ochre
+ Alizarin Crimson
+ Cadmium Yellow Pale
+ French Ultramarine

2 *With a stronger mix, paint the starfish again, dotting it with your brush in places. Paint the sand wet-on-wet, using a directional wash to paint around the shapes, and varying the colours as you work. Finally, paint the shadows on the starfish and the stones.*

Seaweed

This is just one of the many varieties of seaweed that you find on the seashore. Seaweeds are many colours; browns, yellows, reds and greens. They are usually very different colours when wet and when dry. Sketch different seaweeds next time you are on the beach, or take them home to sketch.

1 *Draw the seaweed with your 2B pencil.*

2 *Paint the first colours by dropping them into each other wet-on-wet, using your small brush. Let this dry.*

3 *Now paint the dark colour on top of the first wash in places. This gives the seaweed shape and form.*

EXERCISE Paint mackerel

Fish can be beautiful subjects to paint, but to a beginner it might seem daunting to try to capture some of the colours and iridescence. A mackerel is a good example to start with as it has a distinctive silvery sheen and very definite markings that help to identify it.

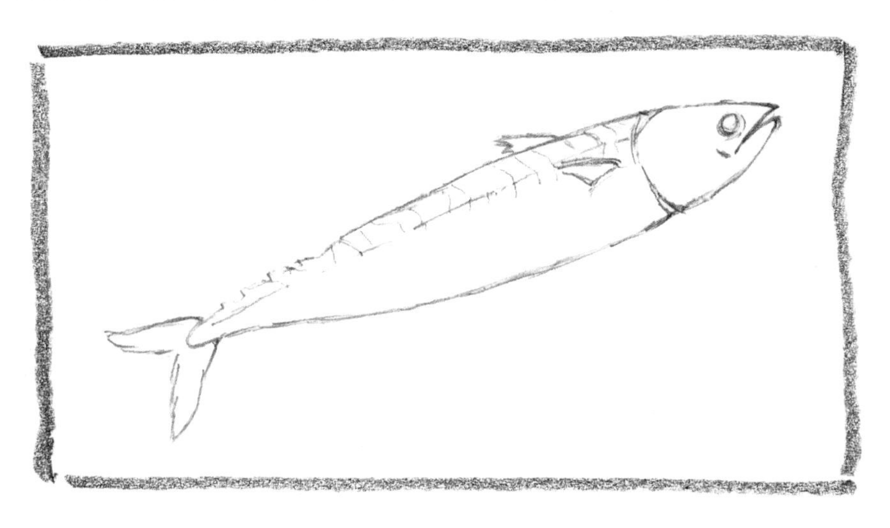

1 *Draw the fish with your 2B pencil. Make sure you capture the long cigar shape, and note the distinctive markings along its back.*

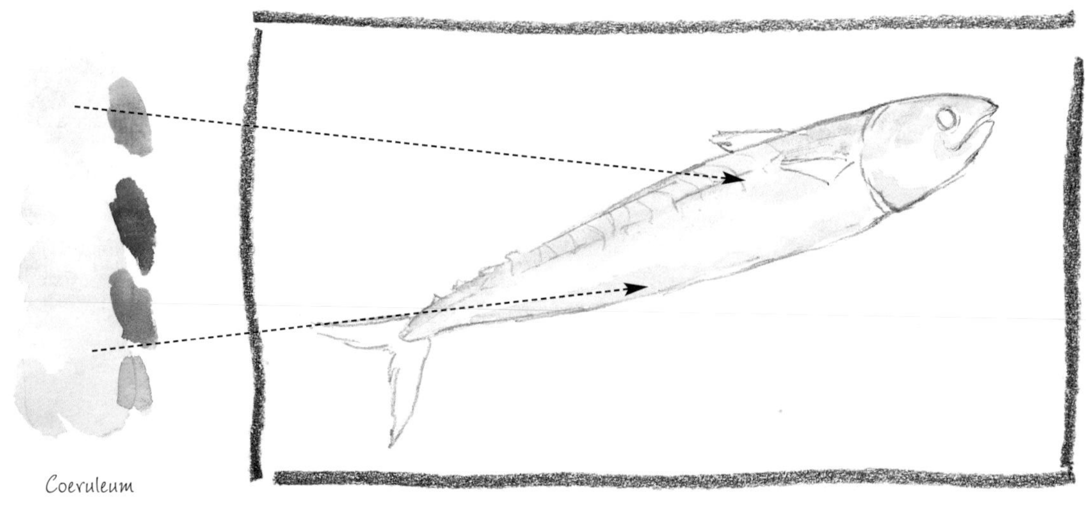

Coeruleum
\+ French Ultramarine
\+ Alizarin Crimson
\+ Yellow Ochre

2 *With your big brush, paint a soft greenish-blue wash on its back. This will start to suggest the iridescence of the sheen on its skin. Now paint a soft pink wash on its underbelly.*

The palette

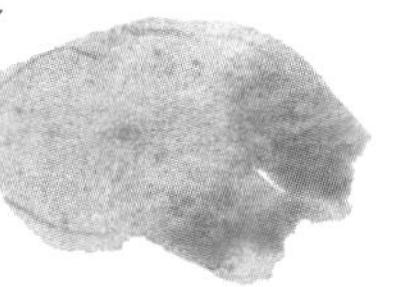

Coeruleum

French Ultramarine

Alizarin Crimson

Yellow Ochre

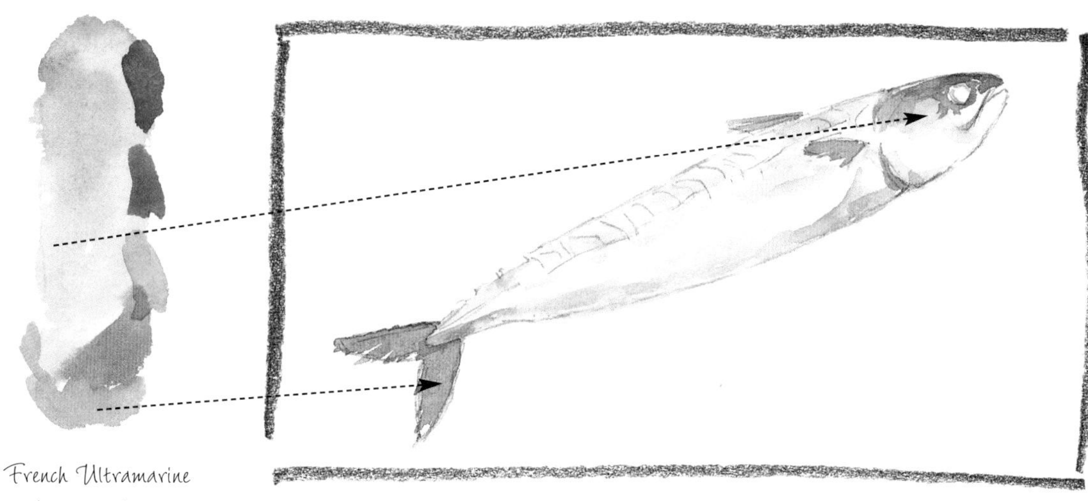

French Ultramarine
+ Alizarin Crimson
+ Yellow Ochre

3 Using your small brush, paint the fins, tail and the gold colour near its eye. When dry, paint dark on the head and soft shadow on its underbelly, which gives more shine to the belly.

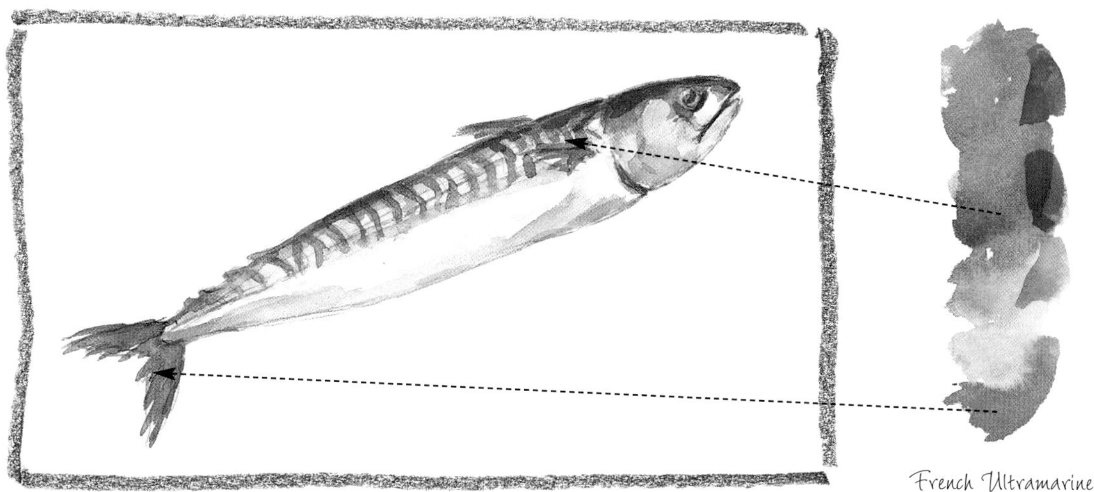

French Ultramarine
+ Alizarin Crimson
+ Yellow Ochre

4 Paint the markings on its back. These identify the fish. With the same colours, paint over the fins and the tail. Add more darks to the head. Finally, paint the eye.

Skies

Skies can be very impressive, and the sky is a very important element when you are painting a seascape. The sky in a painting sets the scene; calm, stormy, hot or cold, you can usually tell what sort of day it is just by the sky and the different cloud formations.

Early evening sky

Study clouds when you are out, and you will soon become familiar with their shapes and formations. This painting looks calm, but there is still plenty of movement high in the clouds, which adds interest to the painting.

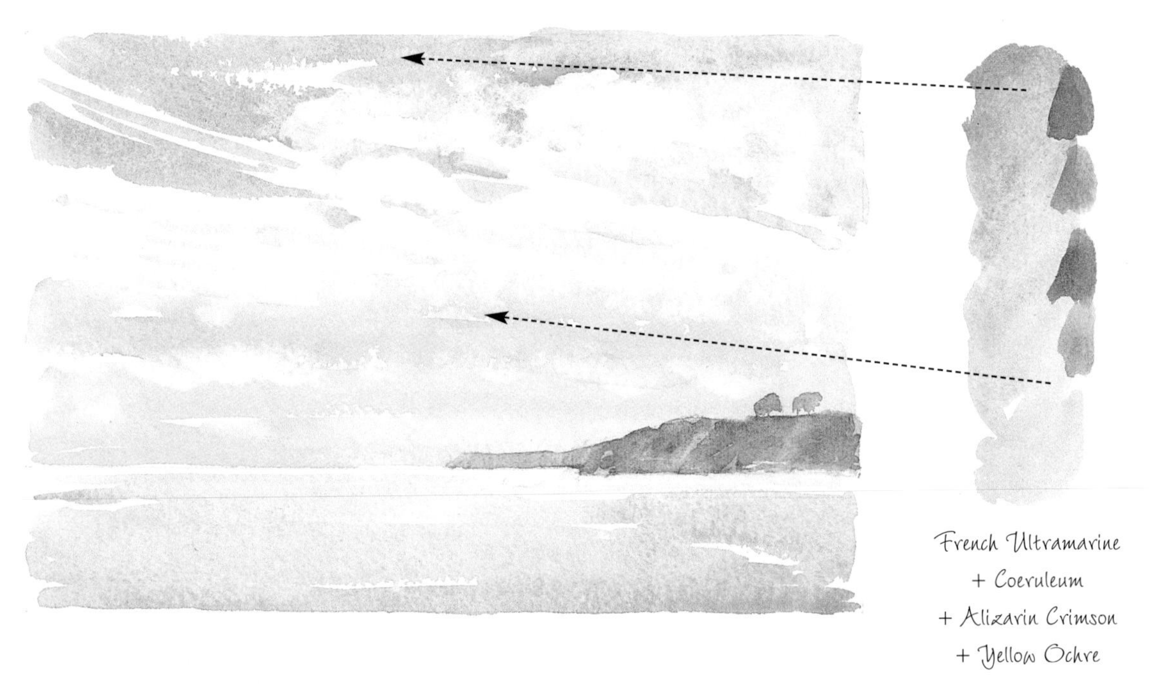

I painted the blue sky leaving white paper to suggest clouds. I used the blotting-out technique to suggest the top clouds. When dry I painted the yellow and pink colours wet-on-wet. The sea was also painted wet-on-wet, leaving a thin white (paper) horizon line. When that was dry I painted the headland. The sky is the most important element in this painting.

Sunlit clouds

This sky has a very different atmosphere to the previous one. The tops of the clouds are very crisp which suggests strong daytime sunlight. You can almost feel the hazy atmosphere where the clouds hit the sea and are reflected in it.

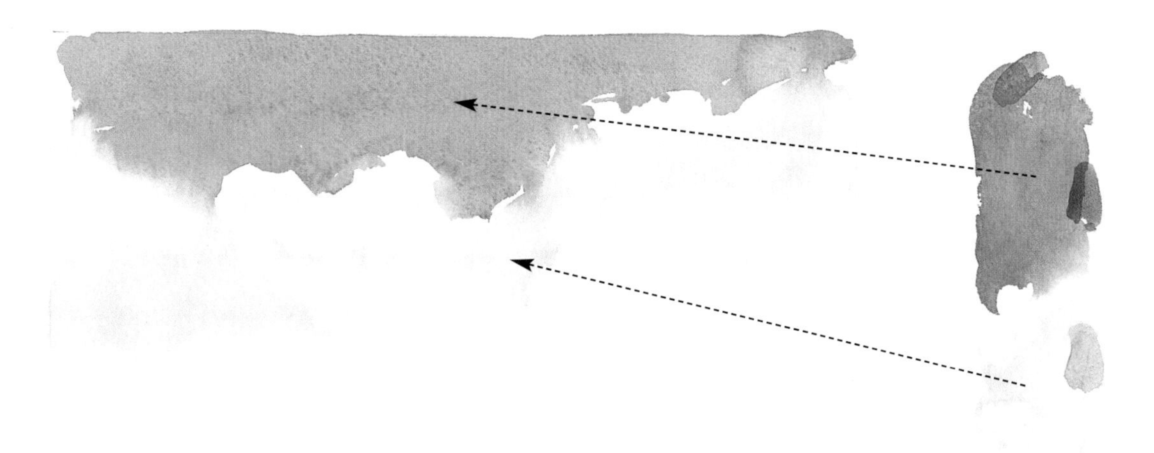

French Ultramarine
+ Alizarin Crimson
+ Yellow Ochre

1 Using your large brush, paint the blue sky, leaving white paper in the shape of clouds. Then, with watery yellow paint, put in the clouds, letting the yellow touch the wet blue sky in places.

French Ultramarine
+ Alizarin Crimson
+ Yellow Ochre

2 Continue, adding shadow colour to the yellow clouds into the blue below. This is all painted wet-on-wet. Notice how leaving areas of unpainted white paper gives life to the painting.

Late afternoon clouds

The sky on the previous page is crisp and sunny. This sky has a much softer, late afternoon look about it. I have used the blotting-out technique for this effect. The horizontal shadows on the clouds give the sky perspective and lead your eye through the painting to the horizon.

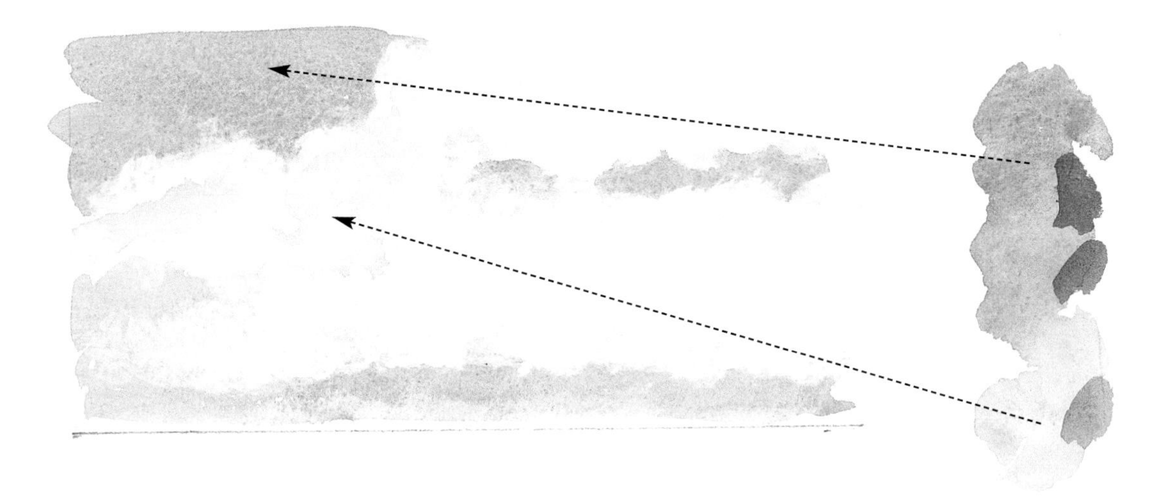

French Ultramarine
+ Alizarin Crimson
+ Yellow Ochre

1 *Using your large brush, paint in the blue sky, leaving some white unpainted paper, and use the blotting-out technique to soften the edges of the clouds. Now add the soft yellow colour.*

French Ultramarine
+ Alizarin Crimson
+ Yellow Ochre

2 *Using your small brush, paint the shadows on the clouds and the pink on the horizon. Paint the sea using the dry-brush technique: this leaves areas of white paper showing the sun sparkling on the water.*

Sunset

When painting a sunset, beware! Don't choose a vividly coloured one as it will look unreal in a painting. Nature can get away with the bright colours, but not many artists can. So either choose a softer sunset, or paint it softer than it really is.

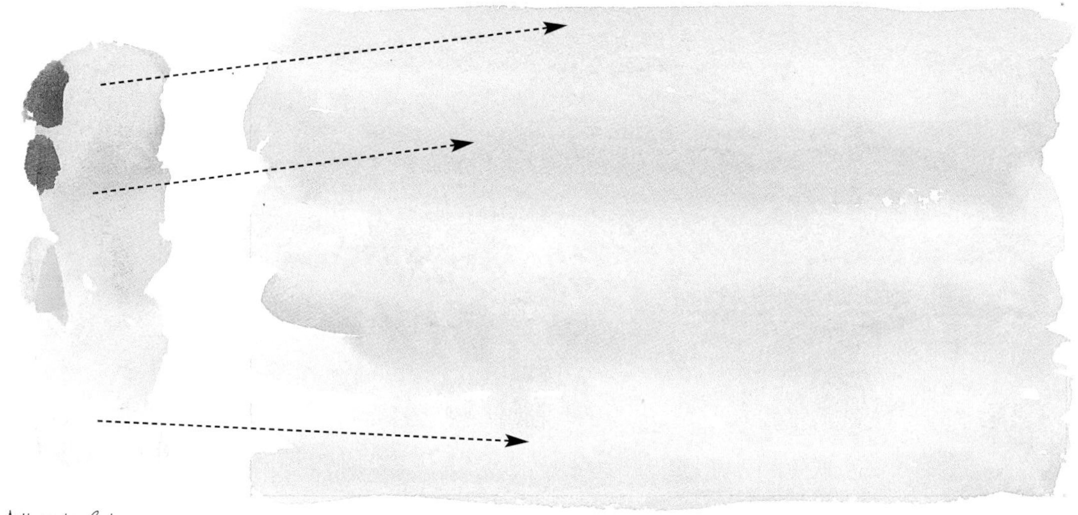

Alizarin Crimson
+ French Ultramarine
+ Yellow Ochre
+ Cadmium Yellow Pale

1 *Paint the background with your large brush using a graded colour wash. Let this stage dry.*

Yellow Ochre
+ Alizarin Crimson
+ French Ultramarine

2 *Now paint in the clouds. Be positive. Let the paint run down to the horizon, wet-on-wet. When dry, paint in the land. Notice how bright the yellowish sun area looks after the land is painted.*

EXERCISE Paint billowing clouds

These billowing clouds certainly make an exciting painting. They are mainly painted wet-on-wet. You need to follow the cloud shapes carefully, leaving unpainted paper around their shapes, or the clouds will disappear.

1 *Draw the shape of the clouds with your 2B pencil and use your large brush to paint the yellow areas.*

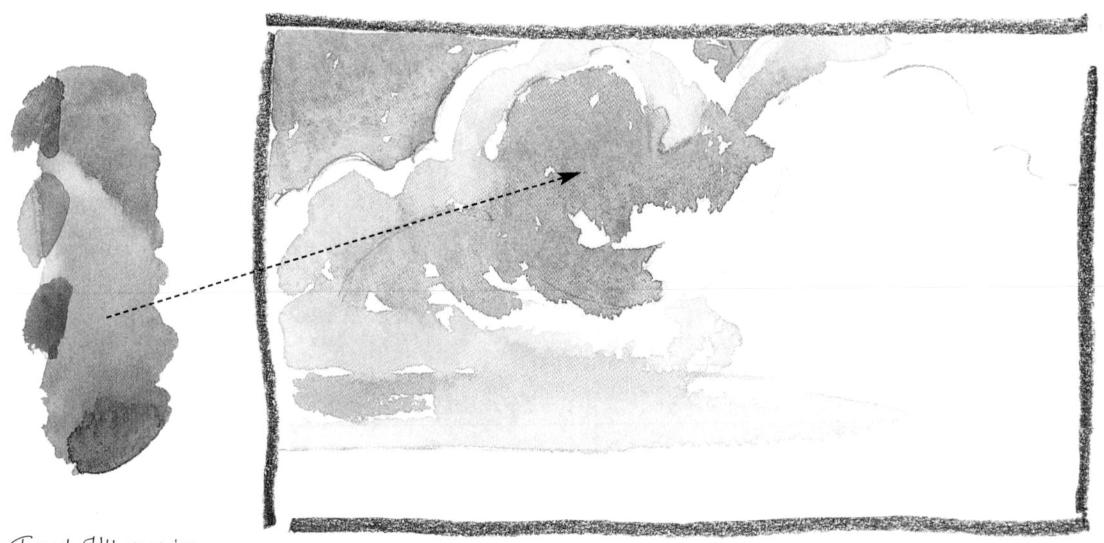

2 *While this is wet, paint in the warm shadow colour, leaving white paper around the clouds, and running more yellow paint underneath them.*

The palette

Yellow Ochre

Alizarin Crimson

French Ultramarine

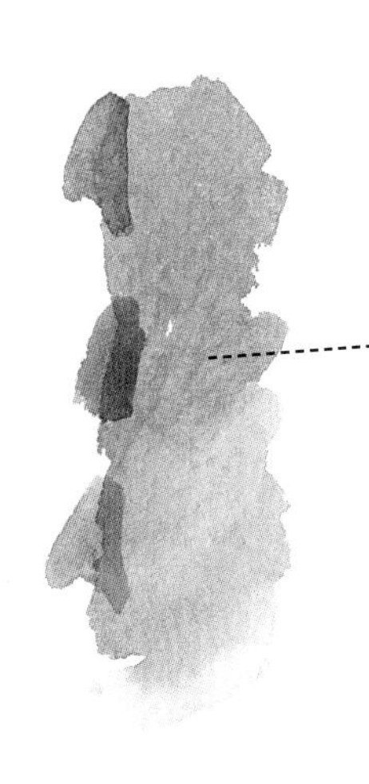

French Ultramarine
+ Alizarin Crimson
+ Yellow Ochre

3 *Continue painting the clouds, adding more blue paint to the dark cloud on the right, still running wet paint into wet paint.*

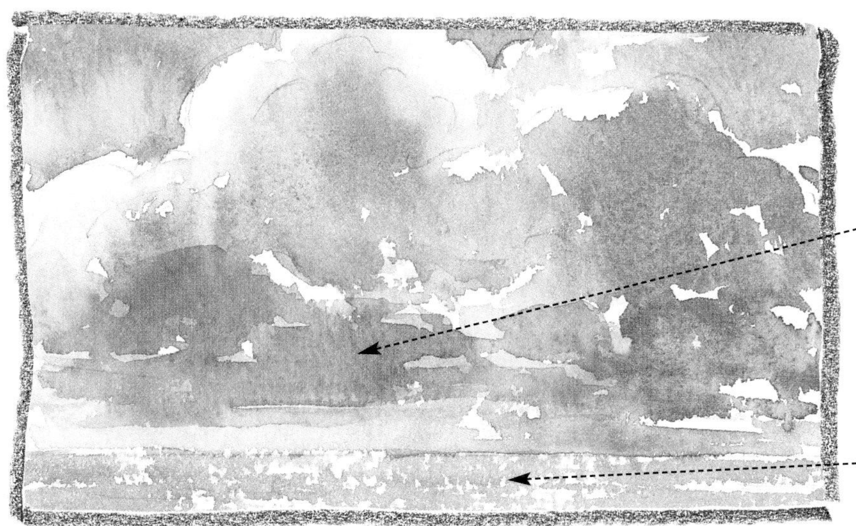

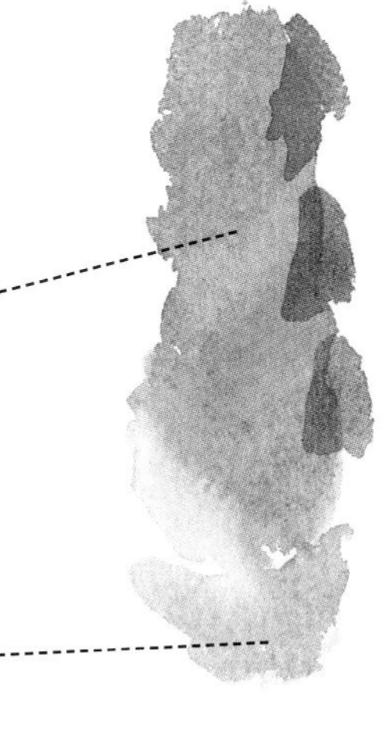

French Ultramarine
+ Alizarin Crimson
+ Yellow Ochre

4 *Add more shadows to the bottom of the clouds. Finally, paint the sea using the dry-brush technique.*

SEAS

I love painting water, especially the sea. Its moods and colours change constantly. From a large seascape to a close-up of a wave, it is an inspiring and challenging subject. Enjoy copying my exercises; they will give you a glimpse of the many opportunities the sea has to offer an artist.

Swelling sea

This painting shows the many colours and patterns that you can get in the sea. The colours change with the reflections on the sea, when the sunlight is shining through it. The colours also vary depending on what is underneath the surface.

I painted the sea first, leaving the girl, the boat and the movement lines in the water as unpainted paper. When dry, I painted the girl and the boat and then the reflections on the water. When this was dry I painted in the shadows. Notice the simplicity of the shadow on the girl and of the water itself: don't be tempted to overwork it.

Waves breaking on a beach

Waves can change colour and shape according to the weather, the type of sea bed lying underneath and when they are crashing onto rocks. Always leave plenty of white paper for the foam, you can paint over it if you have left too much. In this painting, the waves are breaking onto a beach.

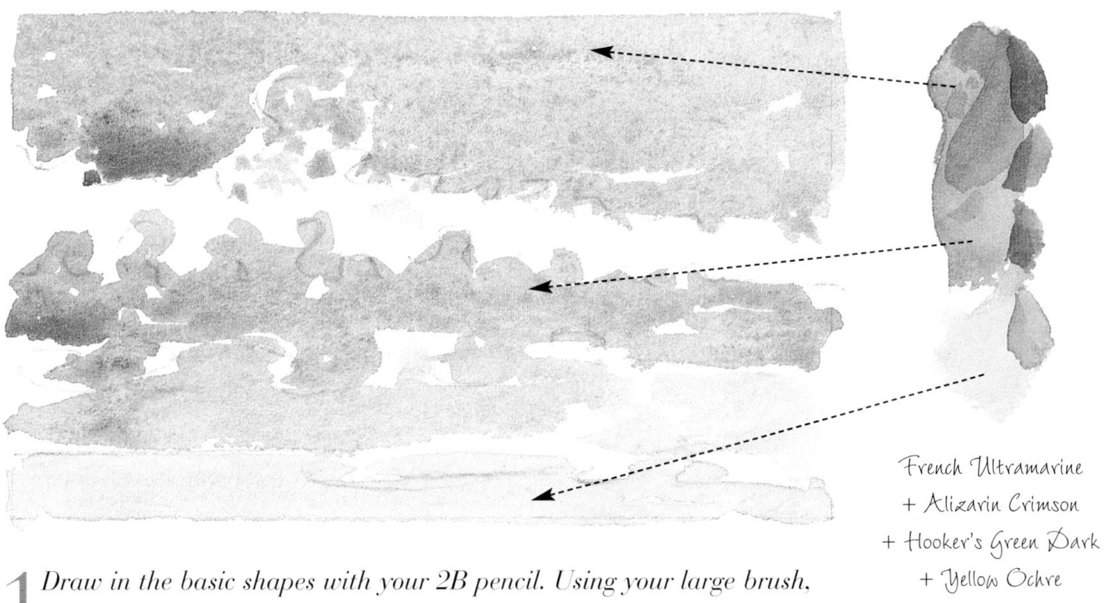

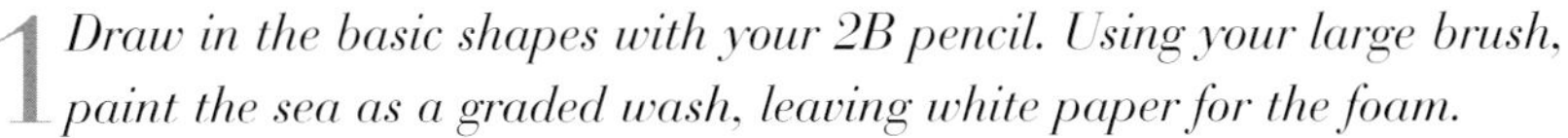

1 *Draw in the basic shapes with your 2B pencil. Using your large brush, paint the sea as a graded wash, leaving white paper for the foam.*

2 *When dry, mix a shadow colour. Paint behind the wave, leaving some underpainting showing. Continue painting shadows on the wave. Finally, soften some areas by lifting out.*

Calm sea

This is a totally different sea to the one on the previous page. The sea is more the colour found around a tropical island, and the atmosphere is calm and tranquil. This is a perfect example of water painted very simply, without overworking.

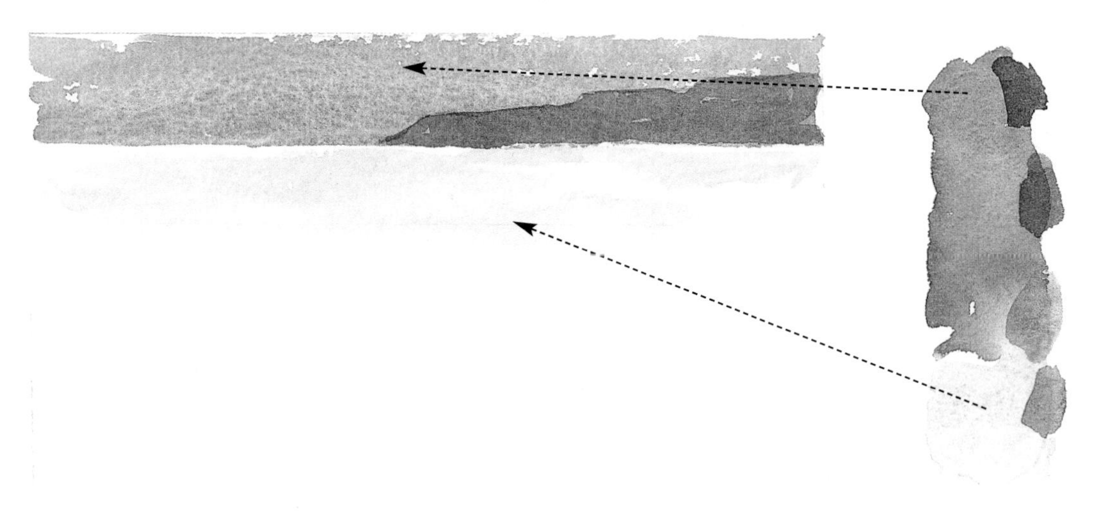

1 *Paint the sky using your large brush. When it is dry, paint the headland with your small brush. Let that dry, then start painting a wash for the sea.*

French Ultramarine
+ Alizarin Crimson
+ Coeruleum
+ Yellow Ochre

Coeruleum
+ Yellow Ochre
+ Alizarin Crimson

2 *Continue painting the sea, leaving white paper for the waves. Paint the sand, leaving some unpainted lines leading to the sea. When dry, paint in the horizontal shadows under the waves.*

Waves crashing on rocks

This is a lively scene with waves crashing onto rocks, throwing up lots of spray. The colour of the sea, the sparkling white of the waves and the dark rocks make the painting vibrant, and the contrast of the very dark areas with the white paper adds dimension and drama.

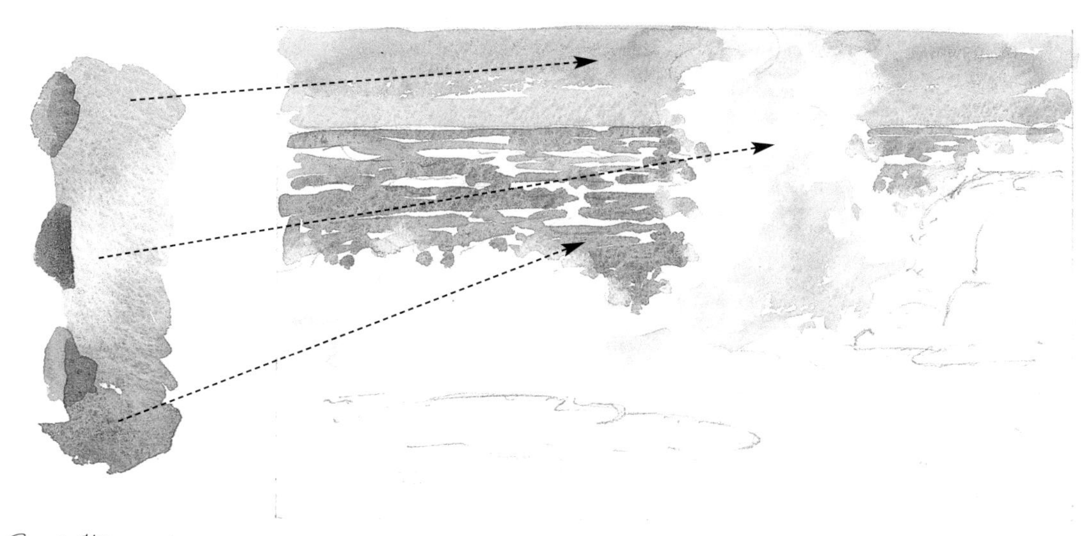

French Ultramarine
+ Alizarin Crimson
+ Hooker's Green Dark

1 Draw in with your 2B pencil. Paint the sky with your large brush, leaving the wave unpainted. Then paint the sea, leaving small white horizontal areas for the background waves. Add soft shadows to the spray.

French Ultramarine
+ Alizarin Crimson
+ Hooker's Green Dark

2 Paint the dark rocks, leaving little specks of white paper to suggest spray. Paint darker areas on the spray, wet-on-wet. Then paint the sea around the rocks with horizontal brush strokes.

EXERCISE Paint a seascape

When you paint this scene, the first two stages are painted while the paint is still wet, so don't stop in the middle, just keep going. Your colours may vary from mine, because they will merge differently when they are wet.

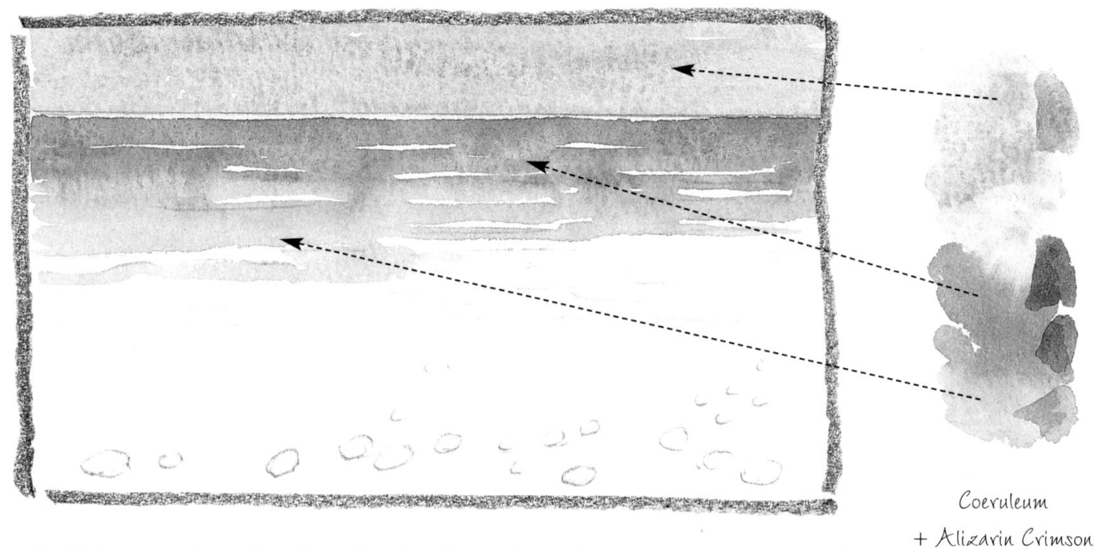

Coeruleum
+ Alizarin Crimson
+ French Ultramarine
+ Yellow Ochre

1 *Using your large brush, paint the sky and sea, leaving a thin unpainted line on the horizon. This prevents the sea merging into the sky.*

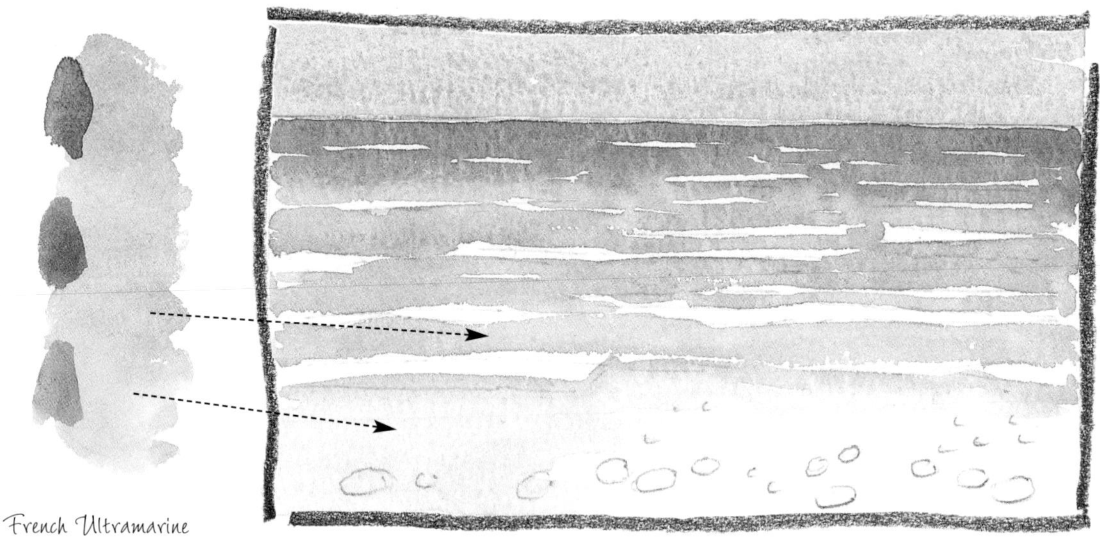

French Ultramarine
+ Alizarin Crimson
+ Yellow Ochre

2 *Continue to paint the sea and the sand, using the graded wash technique. Leave horizontal white paper lines for the waves.*

The palette

Coeruleum

French Ultramarine

Alizarin Crimson

Yellow Ochre

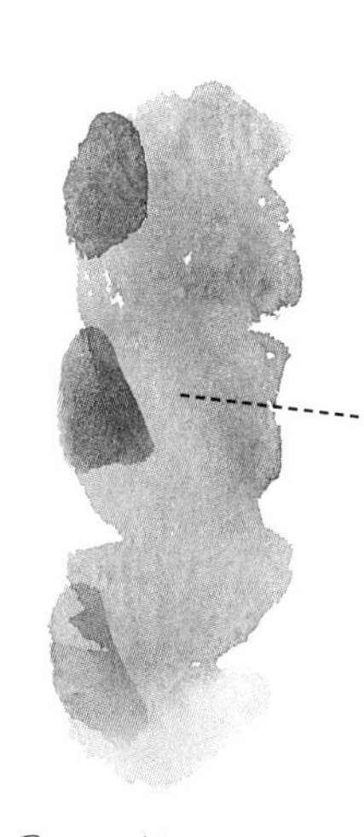

French Ultramarine
+ Alizarin Crimson
+ Yellow Ochre

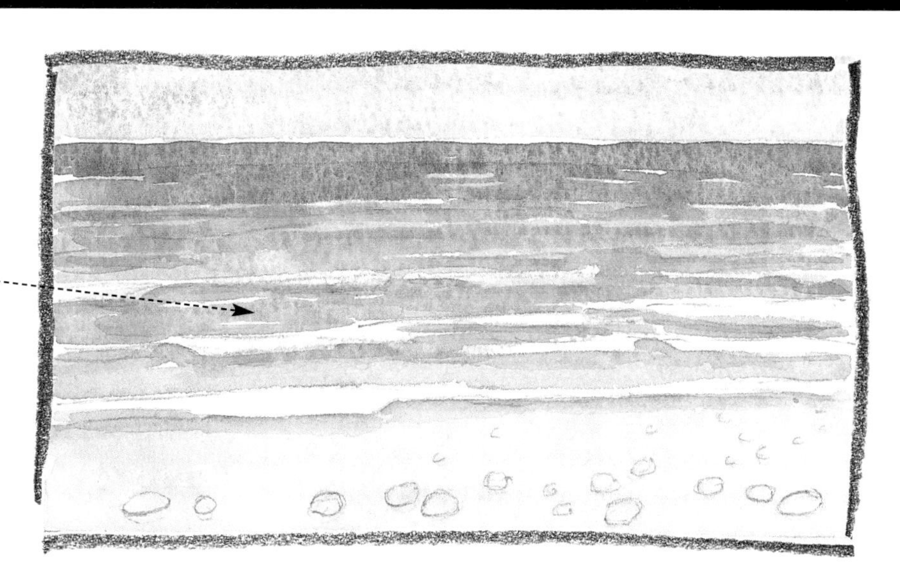

3 *Finish painting the sand. When it is dry, paint the shadows under the waves. Leave to dry.*

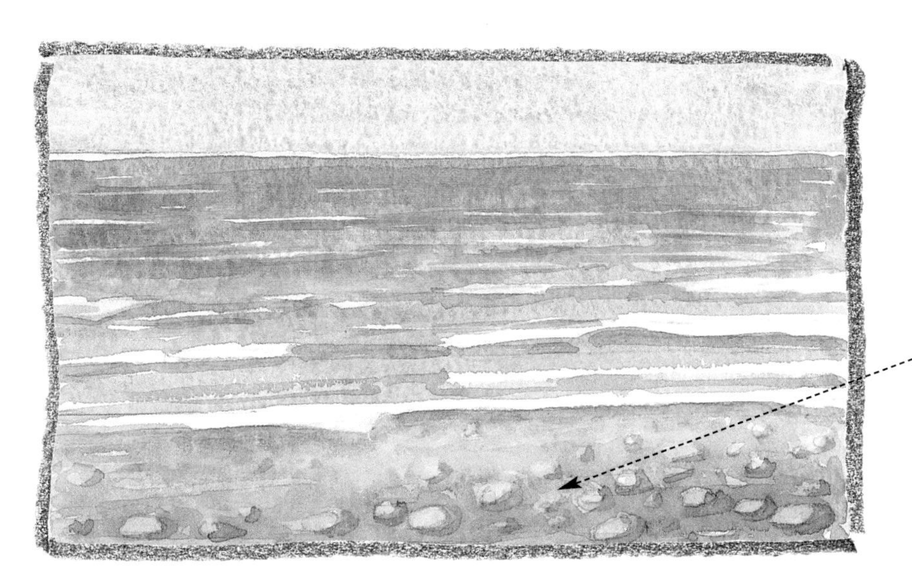

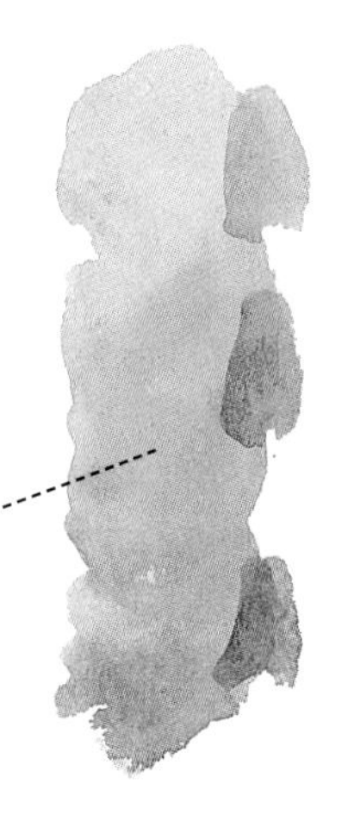

Yellow Ochre
+ Alizarin Crimson
+ French Ultramarine

4 *Use your small brush to paint in the darker sand, leaving the stones pale yellow. When this is dry, paint in the shadows on the stones.*

Cliffs and rocks

Cliffs and rocks play a very important role when you are painting the seashore. They give scale and stability to a seascape painting. They can also help you to paint a recognizable place, especially if they have very distinctive shapes. Cliffs also vary in colour depending on the underlying rock.

Cliffs in silhouette

This is one of many ways of painting cliffs, looking towards the sun. The cliffs become silhouettes and the sea is so bright, it is almost white. You can hardly see the green of the trees and fields on the cliff, and the cliff itself is too dark in shadow to see its colours.

I painted the sky wet-on-wet, changing the colours and worked over the cliffs. I added more water and more Alizarin Crimson and painted the sea, using the dry-brush technique, and worked down into the rocks and beach. When this was dry I painted the cliffs, the jetty on the right and the rocks. Finally, when this was dry, I added shadows.

Distant cliffs

Look carefully at the shapes and colours of cliffs before you start to draw and paint them. Just a few minutes spent looking and observing all the details will help your painting to be believable and give you confidence.

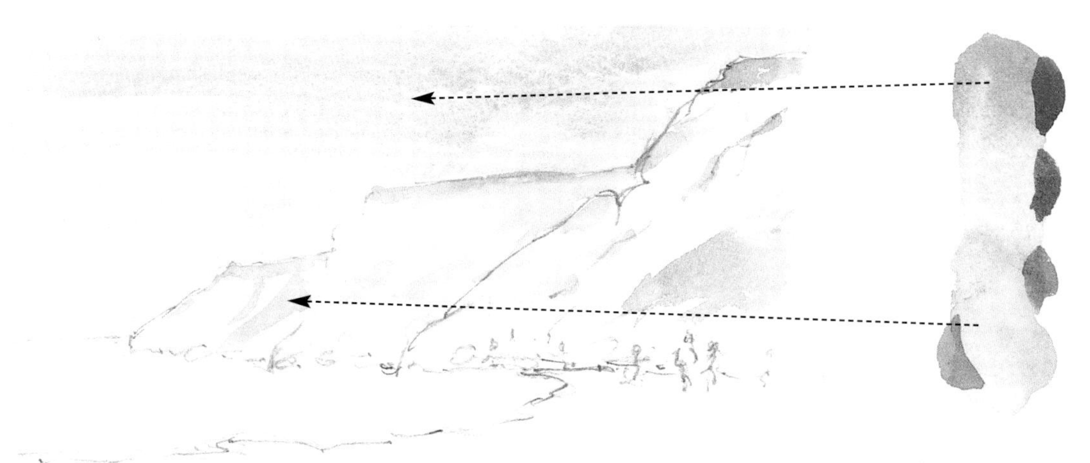

French Ultramarine
+ Alizarin Crimson
+ Hooker's Green Dark
+ Yellow Ochre

1 *Draw the scene with your 2B pencil. Paint the sky with your large brush, going over the far cliff and the sea using the dry-brush technique. Paint the greens on the cliffs, using warmer colours on the nearest cliff.*

French Ultramarine
+ Alizarin Crimson
+ Yellow Ochre
+ Hooker's Green Dark

2 *When dry, use your small brush to paint soft, warm shadows on the far cliff, bluer on the middle cliff and add more red and green paint on the nearest cliff, leaving white shapes for the figures. Add more colour to the sea and sand. Finally, paint the figures.*

Rocks

Rocks are in some ways just small versions of cliffs, or big versions of stones. The rocks in this painting are quite brightly coloured. In some places you will find they are grey, black or even green where seaweed has stuck to them.

1 *Draw the scene with your 2B pencil, and then paint the rocks using your small brush, leaving a thin unpainted line between them, so that the colours won't run from one rock into another.*

2 *When dry, paint in the sea, and then the sand.*

3 *Paint in the last rocks, let them dry, and paint the strong shadows and the rock formation lines.*

Rock pool

Rock pools are magical. They are miniature water worlds full of life, and children and adults alike love them. They can be large or very small. The colours vary according to the type of pool, what is in it, and the reflections on it.

1 *Draw the scene with your 2B pencil, then paint the sky using your small brush. Paint in the water, leaving small areas unpainted for highlights.*

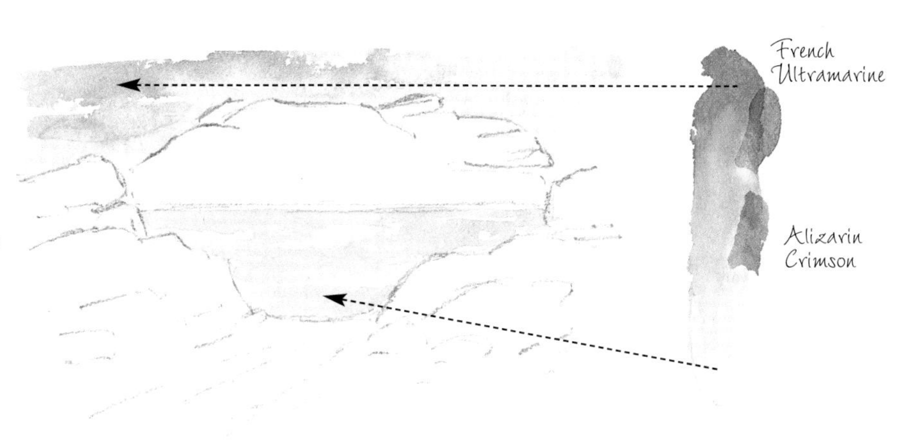

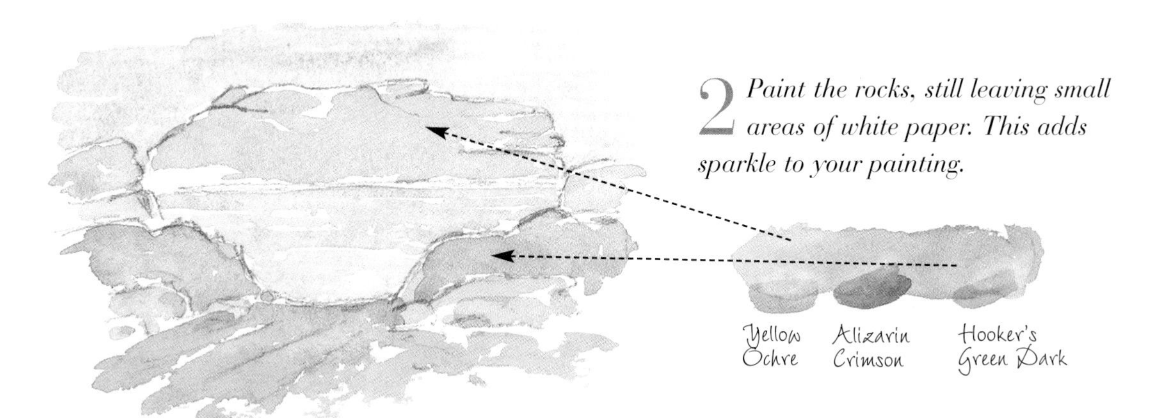

2 *Paint the rocks, still leaving small areas of white paper. This adds sparkle to your painting.*

3 *Paint in the darks on the rocks, making your brush strokes follow their shapes. Finally, paint the dark reflection of the background rock in the water.*

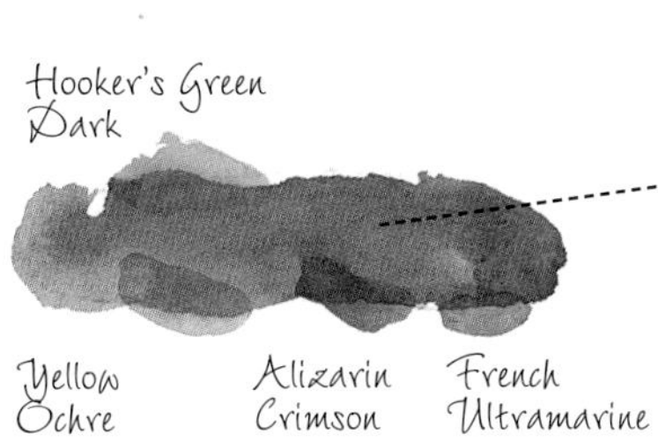

DEMONSTRATION CLIFFS & ROCKS

AT A GLANCE...

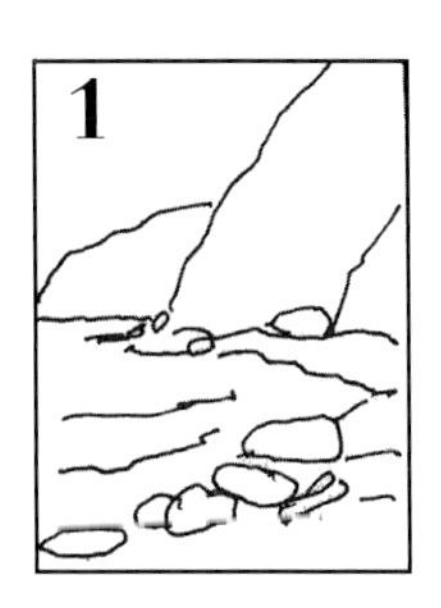

1 *Draw the scene with your 2B pencil. Be positive and free. Note the large foreground rocks; these help to create the impression of distance and dimension. Use my drawing as a guide, but don't try to follow every pencil line.*

2 *Using your small brush, paint a wash for the sky, leaving many small white shapes for seagulls (see page 62). Change the colour, add more water to the paint and work down the sky and over the distant cliffs. Leave to dry.*

The palette

French Ultramarine

Alizarin Crimson

Yellow Ochre

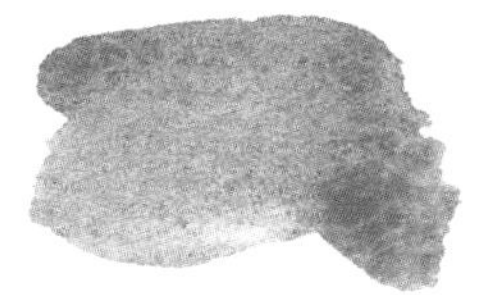
Coeruleum

Hooker's Green Dark

Cadmium Yellow Pale

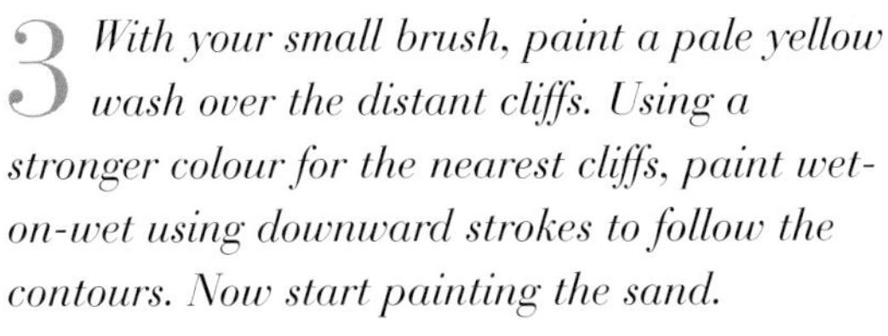
3 *With your small brush, paint a pale yellow wash over the distant cliffs. Using a stronger colour for the nearest cliffs, paint wet-on-wet using downward strokes to follow the contours. Now start painting the sand.*

4 *Continue painting the foreground beach. The curve of the bay before you reach the large rocks in the foreground is very important and helps to balance the picture. Paint the large rocks, changing colours as you work.*

5 *Still using your small brush, paint the sea. Paint a wash, starting with French Ultramarine and a touch of Alizarin Crimson. Leave a thin white paper line and continue with the wash using Coeruleum and a touch of green, varying the colours, and adding more water for the paler green near the beach, until you reach the foreground.*

Detail (actual size): *Look how the colours change. The distant cliff is paler and cooler in colour; the closer cliff has more suggestion of detail and is painted a warmer colour. The sea changes from an Ultramarine blue to a more Coeruleum greenish-blue to a pale green near the beach.*

6 ***Finished picture:*** *Bockingford watercolour paper, 23 x 18cm (9 x 7 in). Mix a shadow colour and paint the modelling on the cliffs. Use a lighter shadow colour in the distance, getting stronger as you get closer. Paint an edge around the sea of the middle shoreline. Now paint the foreground rocks with much stronger shadows, and, finally, paint the dark seagulls.*

SEABIRDS

The most easily recognized sea birds must be the gulls. There are many different types of gulls and you will often see flocks of them soaring in the sky or groups scavenging on the beach. If you include them in your painting they will give life and movement to your seascapes.

Flying gulls

The painting below is very typical of a flock of seagulls 'playing' over the sea. Note how I have painted a dark sky to emphasize the white shapes of the gulls. Don't attempt to add details to them because your eye will be drawn to individual birds rather than seeing the flight of the whole flock.

I drew the gulls with a 2B pencil. I then painted the sky around them wet-on-wet. I left specks of unpainted paper to give the impression of distant gulls. I then painted the gulls with soft shadows. When this was dry, I painted their legs and the tips of their wings.

Black-headed gull

When they are flying, birds are usually very graceful. But sometimes, especially if they are walking, they can look very comical, like the one painted here. He has a rather quizzical expression, as if he is asking for food.

1 *Draw the gull quite carefully with your 2B pencil to get the shape right. Then paint around it with your small brush, wet-on-wet. Let this dry.*

Alizarin Crimson
French Ultramarine

2 *Next paint the head, leaving the eye white. Paint the wings, and then paint in the soft shadow down the front of the bird.*

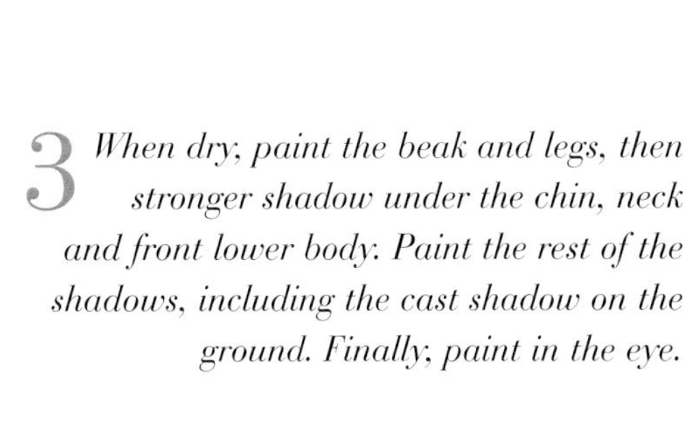

3 *When dry, paint the beak and legs, then stronger shadow under the chin, neck and front lower body. Paint the rest of the shadows, including the cast shadow on the ground. Finally, paint in the eye.*

Curlew

Curlews are very distinctive with their long curved beaks and long legs. This is a lovely shape to draw with long, flowing lines from the beak down under the chest and over the top of the beak to the tail. Comical or graceful – I can't make up my mind.

1 *Make sure you draw the shape of the bird carefully so that it can be recognized. Then start painting it with your small brush from the head downwards.*

2 *Let this stage dry, then paint the beak and legs. Start painting the wing and tail markings.*

3 *Finish painting the markings and the eye using your small brush. Then paint the sand and cast shadow.*

Sketching seabirds

Sketching birds out of doors is very difficult. They are constantly on the move and do not pose for long. But it is good practice and fun to have a go at sketching them. Don't worry if you only get parts of them, and don't forget that you can also take photographs and paint from these.

Sketch birds quickly before they go – aren't they fun!

Leave unpainted paper for white plumage.

Use your rigger brush for the legs and beaks.

Try to sketch those intimate moments.

EXERCISE Paint seagulls

A scene like the one below looks very complicated, but much of it is suggested. Take a close look at the flying gulls; only a few of them are complete gull shapes, the rest are bits of white paper. This is how gulls look in the distance, when there are lots of them.

1 *Draw the scene with your 2B pencil. Then, using your small brush, paint the sky, leaving white paper for the flying gulls and making them smaller where the sky meets the sea.*

2 *This stage is all painted wet-on-wet. Continue painting the sky and sea, leaving thin lines for the horizon and the waves. Paint in the sand, leaving the foreground gulls as white paper.*

The palette

French Ultramarine

Alizarin Crimson

Yellow Ochre

French Ultramarine
+ Alizarin Crimson
+ Yellow Ochre

3 Continue painting the sand, and then paint the wings on the three foreground gulls. Paint a soft shadow underneath their bodies. Leave this stage to dry.

Yellow Ochre
+ Alizarin Crimson
+ French Ultramarine

4 Paint the darker sand and then the beaks and legs of the gulls. Paint darker shadows on the gulls and define some of the flying gulls with the same dark colour.

ON THE BEACH

In the summer the beach is full of exciting subjects to paint, from the simplest, such as a windbreak, to the more difficult, such as a donkey. Take each new subject as a challenge and enjoy having a go at painting many different things when you visit the seaside.

Sand dunes

This is part of a larger painting, and shows high sand dunes topped with coarse grasses, and long stretches of sand, which are typical of the coast around where I live. In the summer, families come to the dunes to picnic and holiday.

I painted the distant land and distant people very soft and bluish, which keeps them in the background. I painted the middle figures and windbreaks stronger colours, and the foreground people the strongest, giving depth and distance to the painting. Finally, I added strong shadows to the foreground people and the beach to give the impression of sunlight.

Bucket and spade

In the summer holidays you will see buckets and spades in all shapes and sizes. Putting them into summer beach paintings is a must. They are many colours, so if you need a particular colour in your painting, a bucket and spade could be the answer.

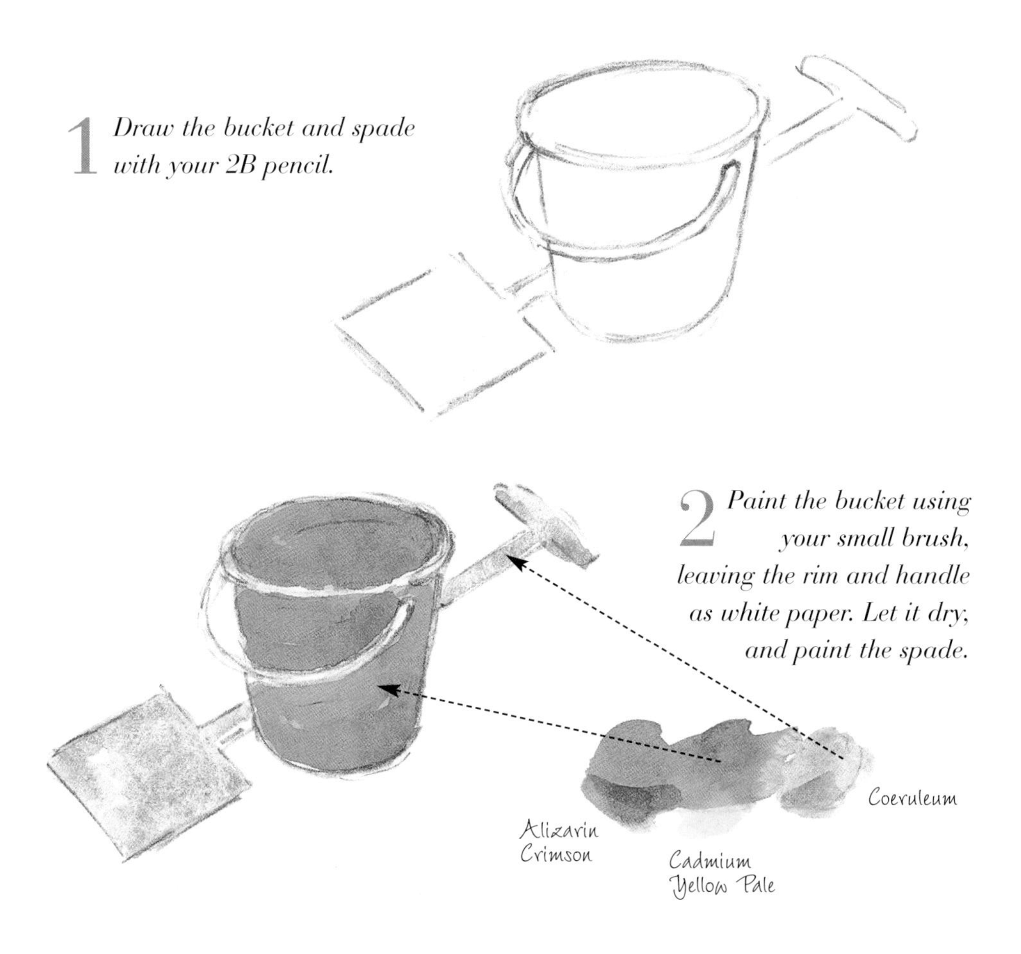

1 *Draw the bucket and spade with your 2B pencil.*

2 *Paint the bucket using your small brush, leaving the rim and handle as white paper. Let it dry, and paint the spade.*

3 *When this is dry, paint the sand. Now paint the shadow in the bucket and on its right-hand side, and on the spade.*

Windbreak

Windbreaks are very much a part of the seaside in summer. They add colour and dimension to a scene. Their colours can be very bright, or soft where they have been faded gently by the sun. The stripes can be any width, but try to keep them flowing and not too uniform.

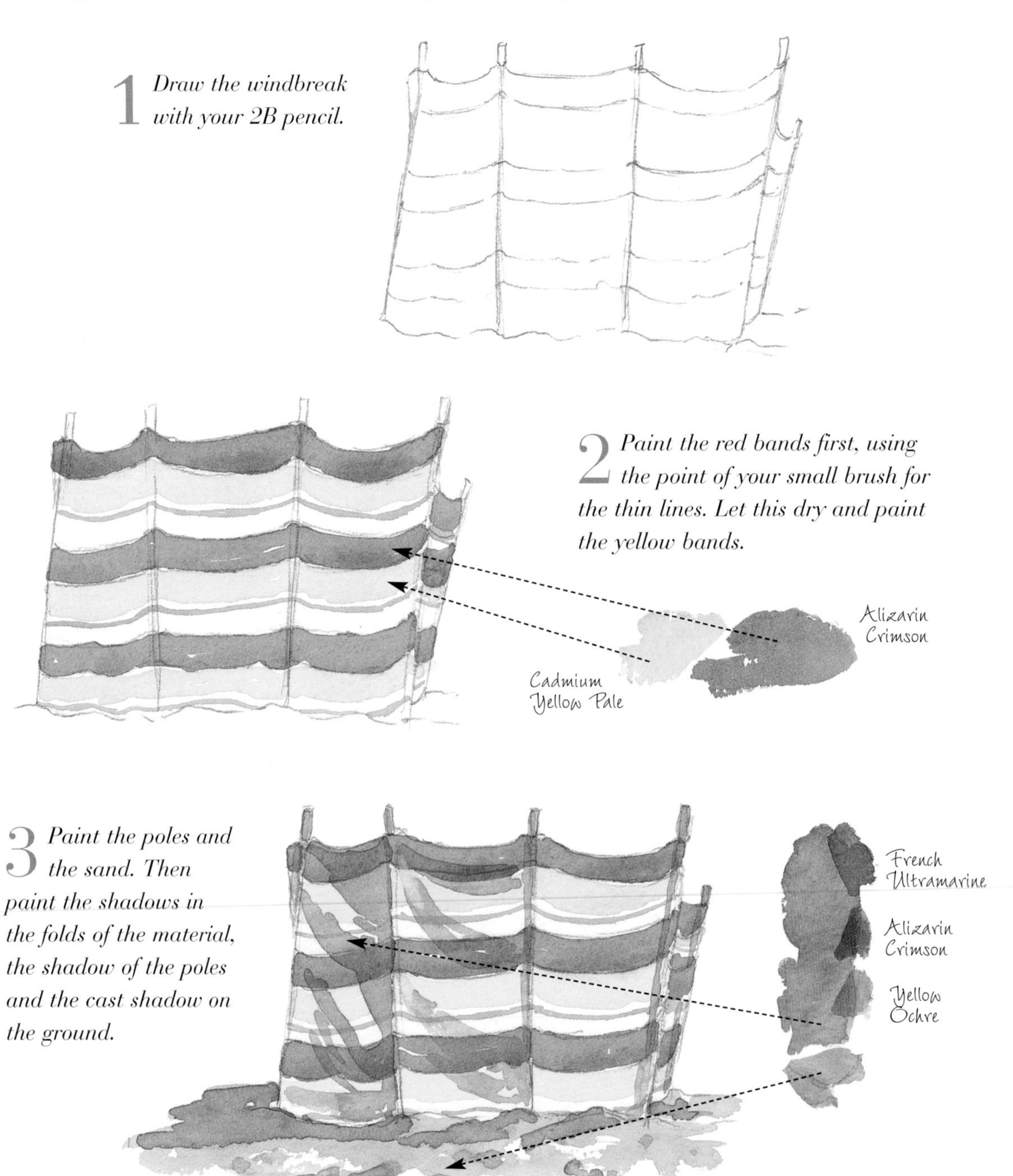

1 Draw the windbreak with your 2B pencil.

2 Paint the red bands first, using the point of your small brush for the thin lines. Let this dry and paint the yellow bands.

3 Paint the poles and the sand. Then paint the shadows in the folds of the material, the shadow of the poles and the cast shadow on the ground.

Deck chair

Deck chairs are all different colours and sizes, but the basic construction is usually the same. Look carefully at the deck chair below and you will see how it works. This will help you when you are out painting them on the beach.

1 *Draw the deck chair carefully with your 2B pencil.*

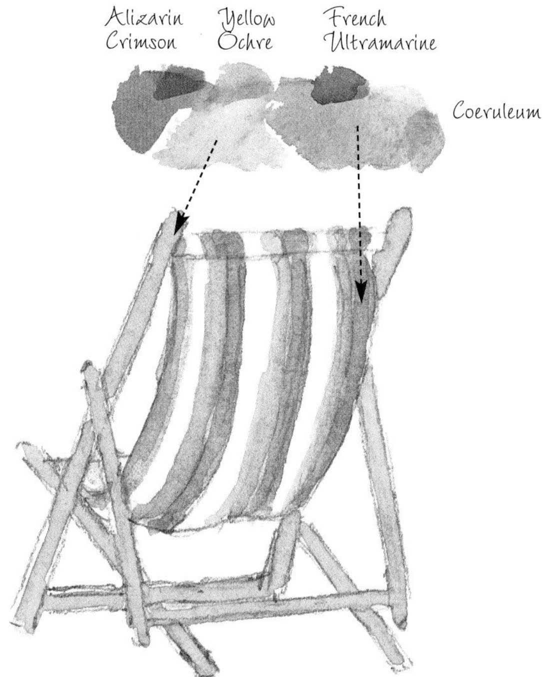

2 *Paint in the blue stripes using your small brush. When dry, paint the yellow stripes. Let these dry, then paint the wood.*

3 *Mix a shadow colour and paint the shadows on the wood.*

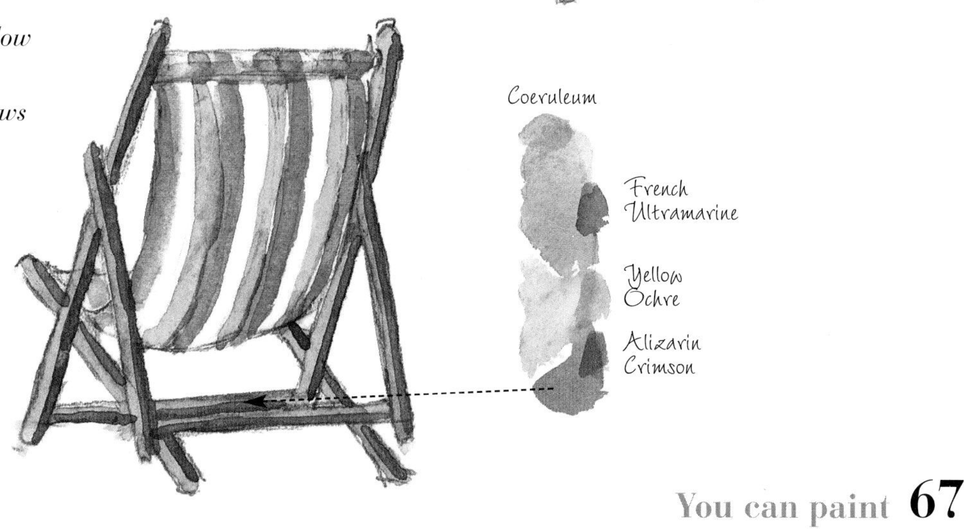

Pebbly beach

Most beaches have some pebbles on them. Look carefully at the scene below, and see how simply the pebbles are painted. Most of them are merely suggested, with the use of magical shadows to make them appear three dimensional.

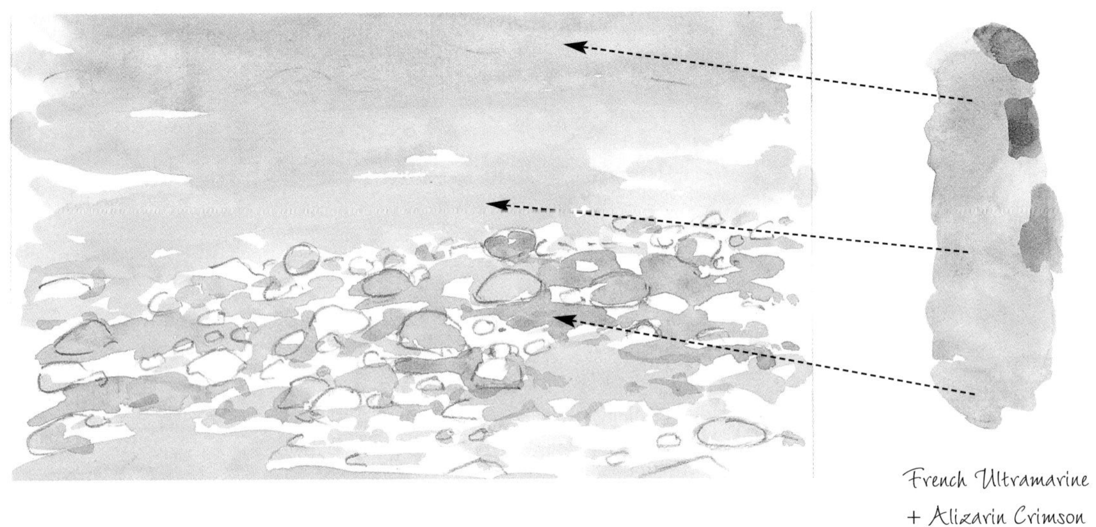

French Ultramarine
+ Alizarin Crimson
+ Yellow Ochre

1 *Draw in a few pebbles with your 2B pencil, then paint the sand using your large brush and leave most of the pebble area as unpainted paper. When this is dry, paint in the grey and pink areas of the pebbles.*

French Ultramarine
+ Alizarin Crimson
+ Yellow Ochre

2 *Let the paint dry, add cast shadows from the pebbles, and paint a few darker pebbles in places. Don't worry about copying my painting exactly; if you are happy with your results, that's fine.*

Breakwater

Breakwaters can make interesting little paintings close up, like the one below, or they can be used as important elements in a larger seascape. They can look very new or may be worn away by the sea to almost nothing. They add interest and scale to a beach painting.

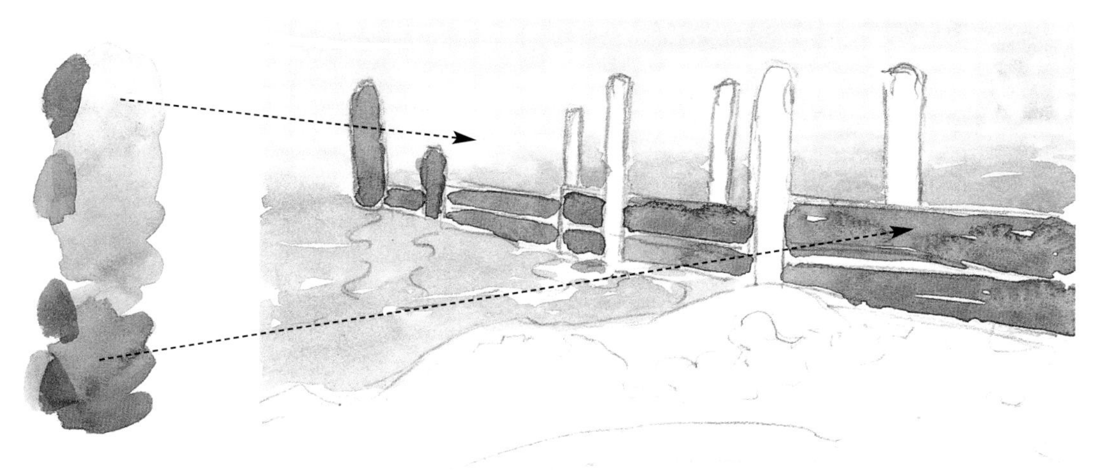

French Ultramarine
+ Hooker's Green Dark
+ Alizarin Crimson
+ Yellow Ochre

1 Using your 2B pencil, draw in the scene. Then use your large brush to paint a blue-grey wash for the sky and the sea. Start painting in the breakwater.

French Ultramarine
+ Hooker's Green Dark
+ Alizarin Crimson
+ Yellow Ochre

2 Continue painting the breakwater. Paint the yellowish wave, leaving white paper for the spray, and continue up the beach. Paint the reflections in the water. Add darks where they are needed.

Beach huts

I love to see beach huts. They are like brightly coloured little houses, and add colour and life to a beach scene. Sometimes they are bleached by the sun and the sea, and look wonderfully weathered. This exercise, of a row of three, shows you how simply they can be painted.

1 Draw the huts with your 2B pencil. Use your small brush to paint them in their different colours. Let them dry.

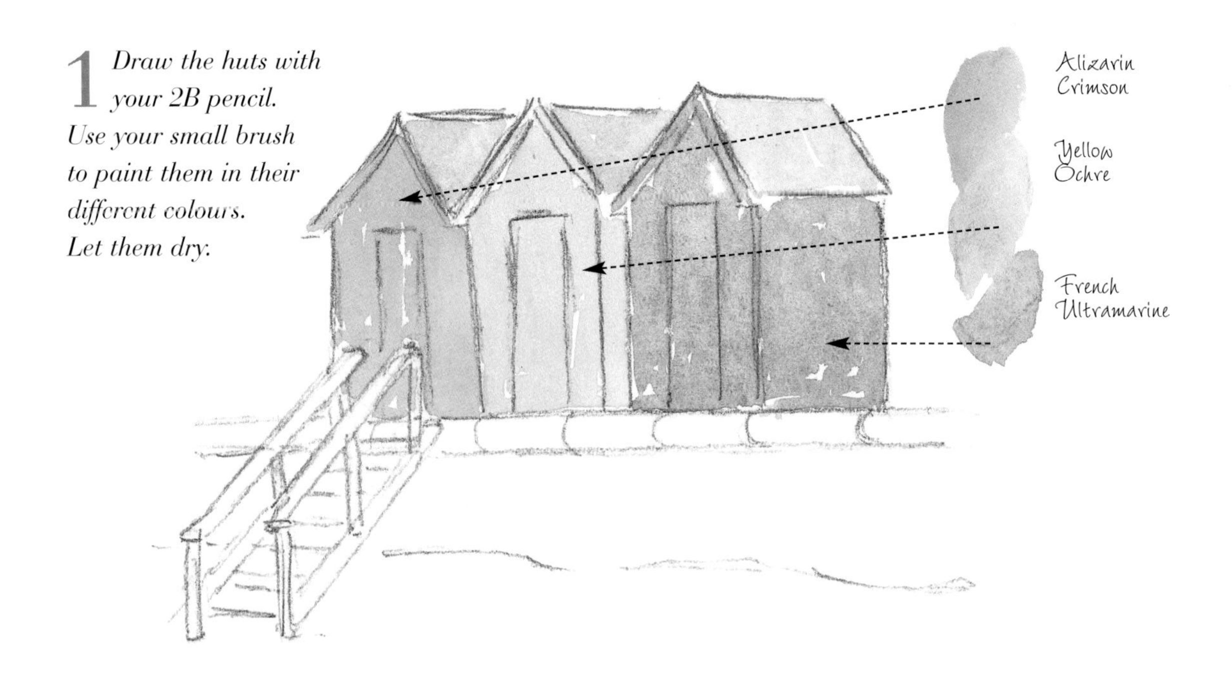

2 Next paint the sea wall, the sand and the steps. When this is dry, paint the dark sides of the huts and extra colour on the doors.

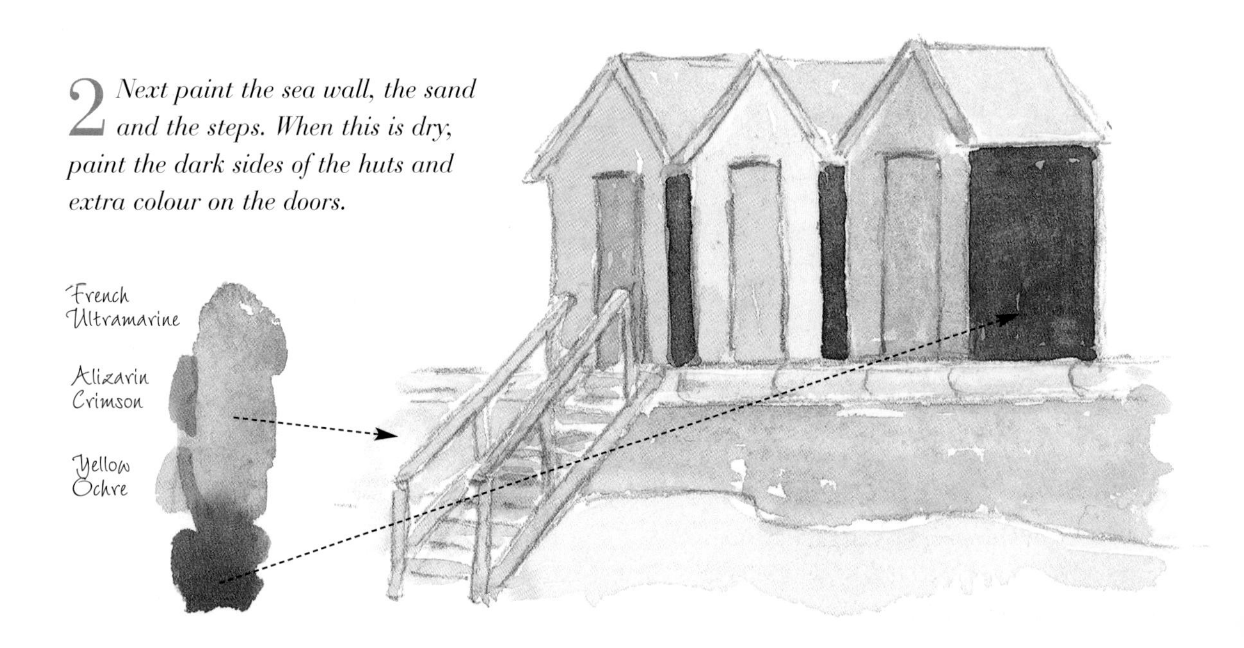

Donkey

Seeing donkeys on the beach conjures up images of childhood – long summer days paddling in the sea, picnics on the beach and donkey rides. To paint donkeys you will need to study them carefully, take photographs, and do plenty of practice.

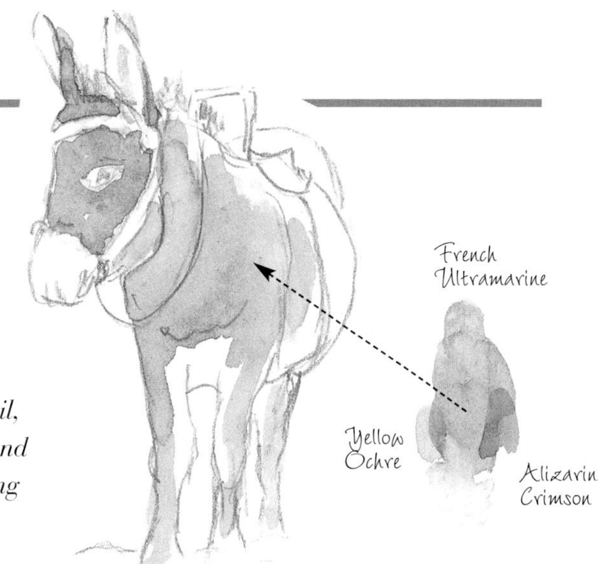

1 *With your 2B pencil, draw the donkey and start the first wash using your small brush.*

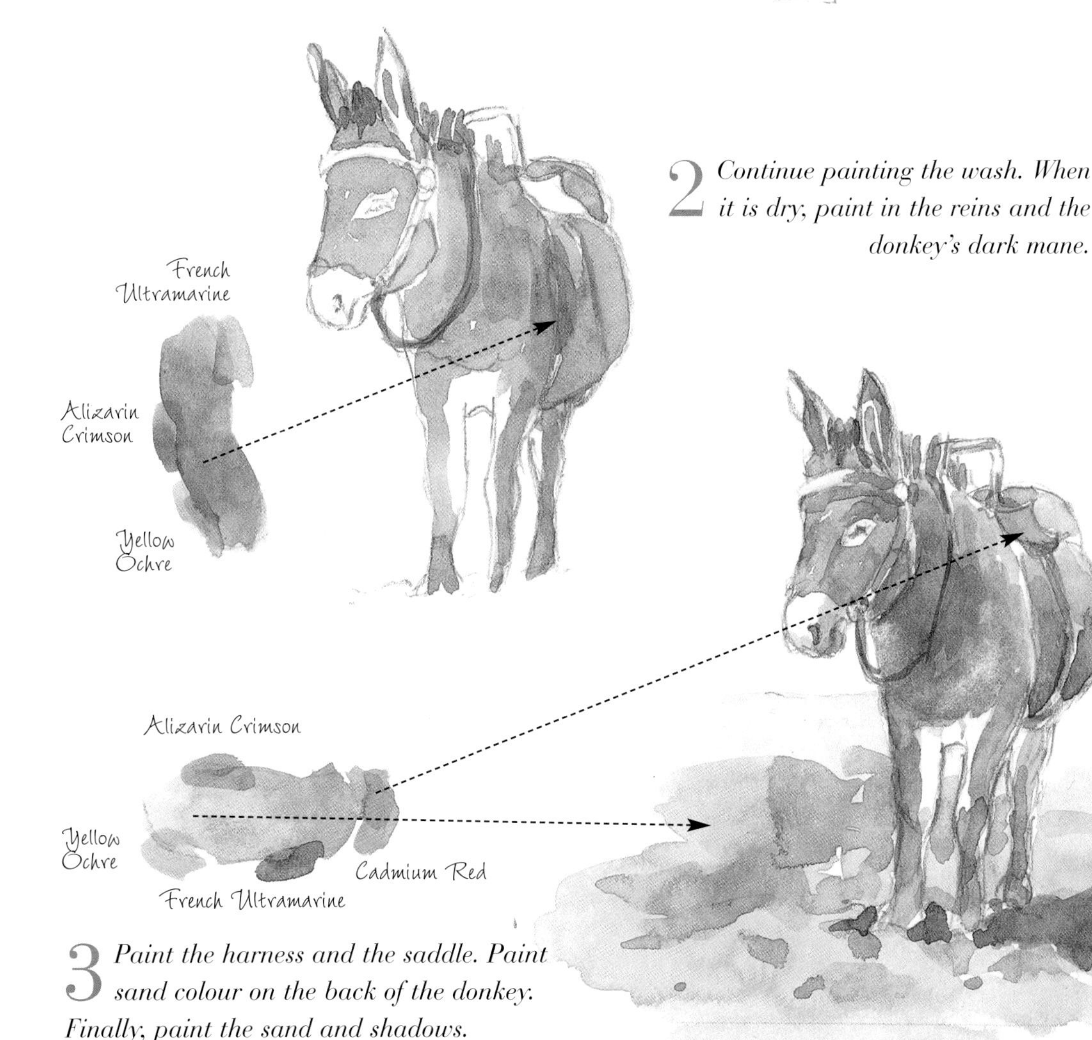

2 *Continue painting the wash. When it is dry, paint in the reins and the donkey's dark mane.*

3 *Paint the harness and the saddle. Paint sand colour on the back of the donkey. Finally, paint the sand and shadows.*

Sketching at the beach

Don't forget to take your sketchbook when you go to the beach. There is always something for you to sketch. Practise by copying these pictures. Notice how the deck chairs, the windbreaks and the beach huts below are painted more freely than those on the previous pages. This is because the sketches are painted as part of a scene and not as objects in their own right.

The shadows cast by these beach huts show that it is a sunny day.

Note how the shadow of the person is visible through the deck chair.

Windbreaks are very simple to sketch and very effective.

These sand castles look three dimensional because of their shadows.

Just one of the many ways to paint a breakwater.

Drawn and shaded with a 2B pencil, then a few simple brush strokes, and here are two donkey riders.

This is a very simple image to sketch.

The sky and sea were painted very simply.

A familiar sight at the seashore.

Don't overlook subjects like this. They make very interesting paintings.

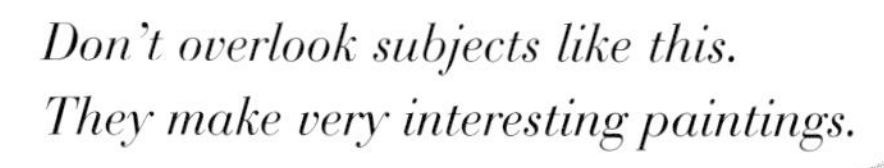

EXERCISE Paint a beach scene

This scene is painted from an unusual viewpoint. I was looking down from the top of the cliff. The breakwaters are a long way down and look quite small. The broken gate is close up which gives the impression of distance. The shadows help to hold the whole painting together.

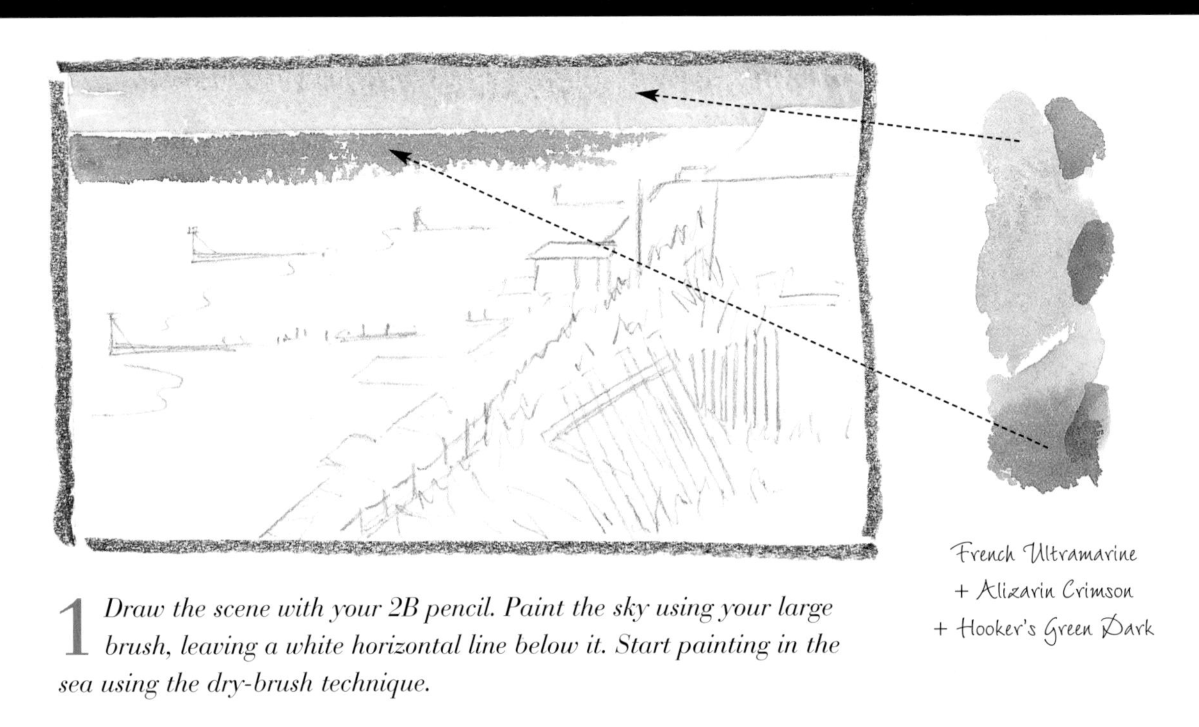

1 Draw the scene with your 2B pencil. Paint the sky using your large brush, leaving a white horizontal line below it. Start painting in the sea using the dry-brush technique.

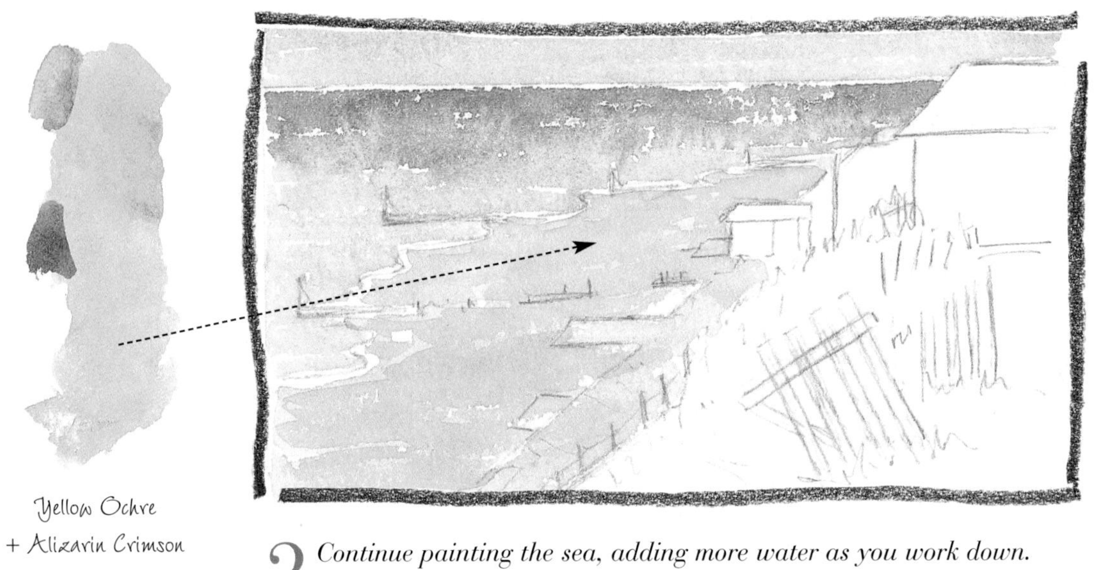

2 Continue painting the sea, adding more water as you work down. Next, paint the sand, leaving white paper for the hut.

The palette

French Ultramarine

Alizarin Crimson

Hooker's Green Dark

Yellow Ochre

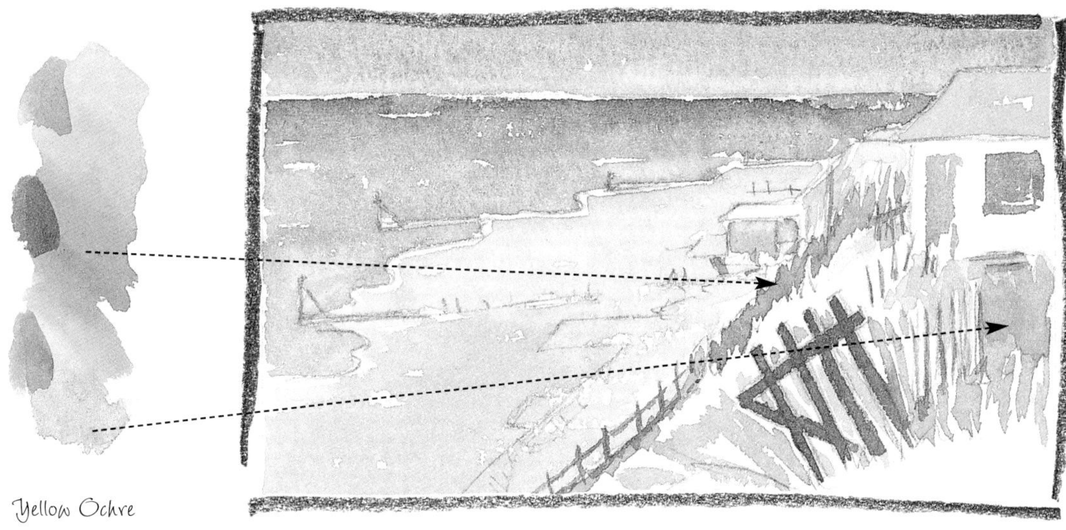

Yellow Ochre
+ Alizarin Crimson
+ Hooker's Green Dark

3 *Using your small brush, paint the pink roof, hut and grasses, then paint in the green grass. When dry, paint the windows on the building and the gate in the foreground.*

French Ultramarine
+ Alizarin Crimson
+ Yellow Ochre

4 *Paint in the fences and breakwaters. When these are dry, paint the shadows from the cliff falling across the beach.*

PEOPLE ON THE BEACH

Seeing people enjoying themselves on the beach – children making sandcastles, people swimming, grandparents watching – makes me feel I must capture all these wonderful scenes. With the help of these exercises I am sure you will soon be able to include people in your watercolour sketches.

Family holiday

I painted this from pencil sketches I had done on the beach. The grandparents and the children are waving to the parents in the sea. I have kept the sea and the figures in the sea very simple. The most important element in the painting is the group in the foreground.

I painted the sea very simply, changing the colours as I worked down and around the figures with horizontal brush strokes, wet-on-wet. When this was dry, I painted the figures, and finally painted in the shadows on the people and the sea.

Placing people on the beach

When painting people on a beach, look for the horizon (this is your eye level). If the beach is level, the horizon will cross the people in the same place on their bodies (see below). Naturally people are different sizes, and the beach isn't always level, but this gives you something to work with.

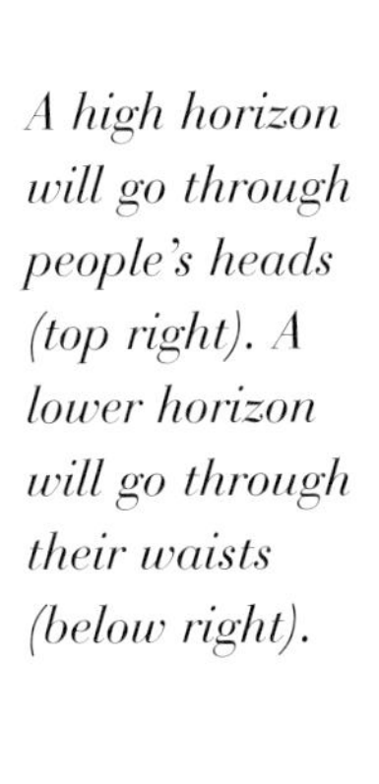

A high horizon will go through people's heads (top right). A lower horizon will go through their waists (below right).

Note how you make people appear further away by painting them smaller and painting their feet further up the beach.

When working out the height of the average person, a general rule is that a figure can be divided from head to foot into approximately seven head lengths, as shown in this blue figure.

Girl in a swimsuit

This exercise shows you how simply you can paint figures. Hair, flesh and again those magic shadows, and suddenly you have a three-dimensional figure. I have deliberately left the swimsuit as white paper to emphasize the simplicity.

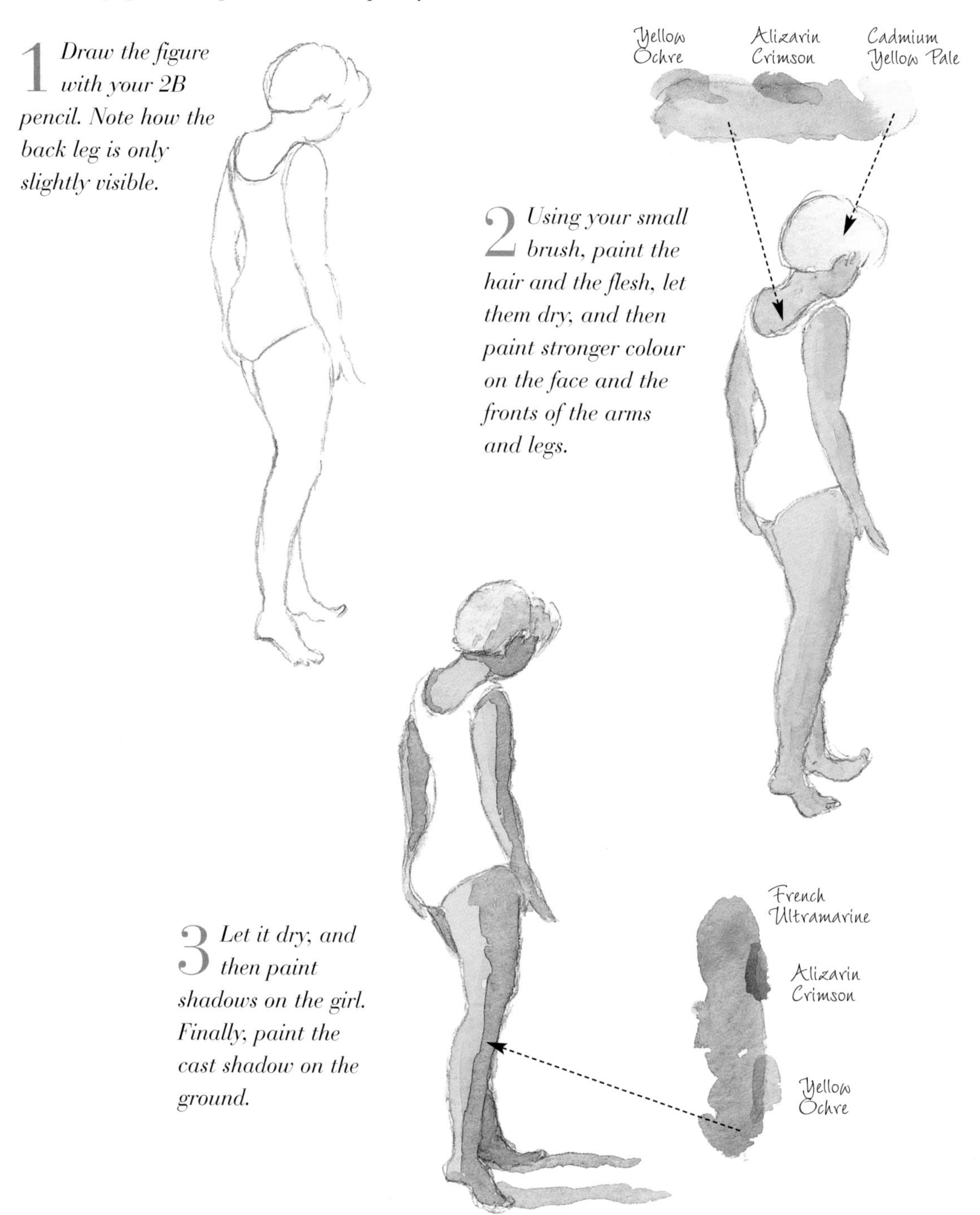

1 *Draw the figure with your 2B pencil. Note how the back leg is only slightly visible.*

2 *Using your small brush, paint the hair and the flesh, let them dry, and then paint stronger colour on the face and the fronts of the arms and legs.*

3 *Let it dry, and then paint shadows on the girl. Finally, paint the cast shadow on the ground.*

Paddler

The shadows and the stance of the boy are very important in this painting. He looks as if he is very relaxed. Notice how the downward curves of the stripes on his shirt emphasize the feeling of relaxation, and the strong shadows give the impression of sunlight.

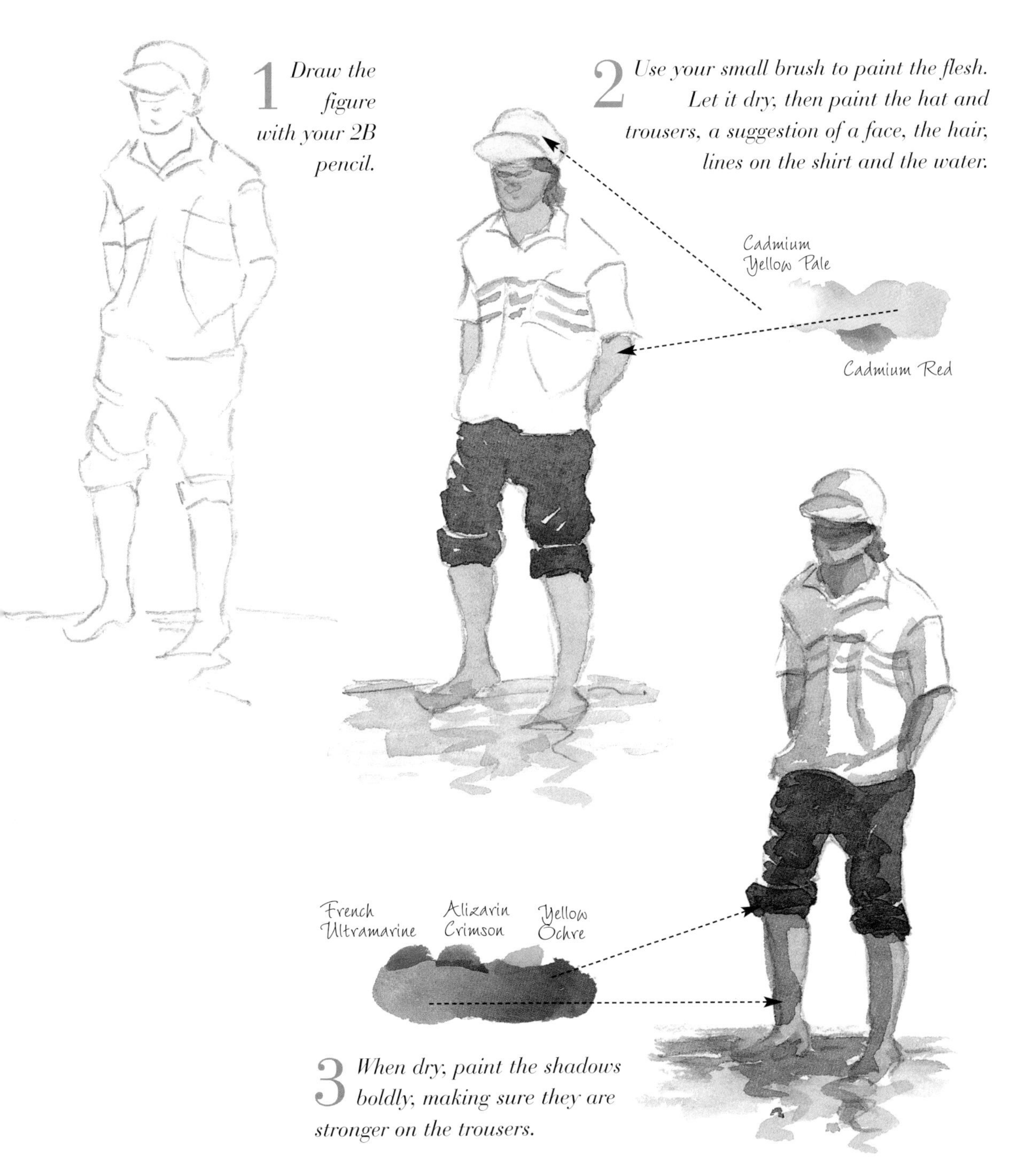

1 *Draw the figure with your 2B pencil.*

2 *Use your small brush to paint the flesh. Let it dry, then paint the hat and trousers, a suggestion of a face, the hair, lines on the shirt and the water.*

3 *When dry, paint the shadows boldly, making sure they are stronger on the trousers.*

Girl playing

Children come in all shapes and sizes, and don't keep still for a minute. Get plenty of practice and use photographs of your or your relatives' children to copy from and you will soon enjoy painting them. This girl is nearly all in shadow, and you can almost feel the sun on her.

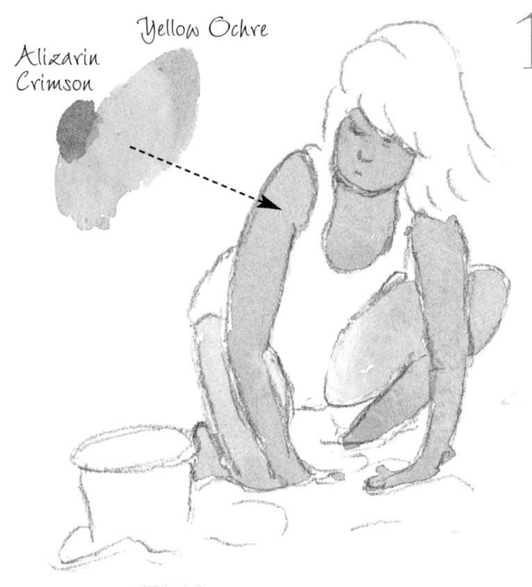

1 *Draw the girl with your 2B pencil. Paint her flesh using your small brush. Add more water to the top of the inside legs to make them paler.*

2 *Let this dry, and then paint the hair, swimsuit and bucket, and let it dry again.*

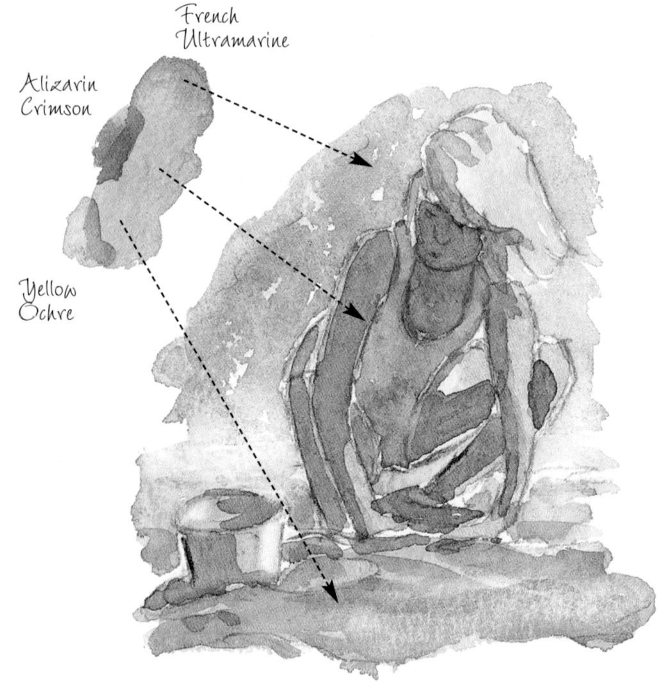

3 *Paint a wash on the background using directional brush strokes. Let this dry. Then paint over the girl's body with a wash of shadow colour, leaving the sunlit areas.*

Group on the beach

As well as all the people sitting and playing on the beach, you will see groups and couples walking. You don't want to put a lot of detail in them, as they are usually part of the scene, and not the main point of interest. Too much detail would make them 'jump out' of the picture.

1 *Draw the figures in freely with your 2B pencil, and use your small brush to paint the flesh.*

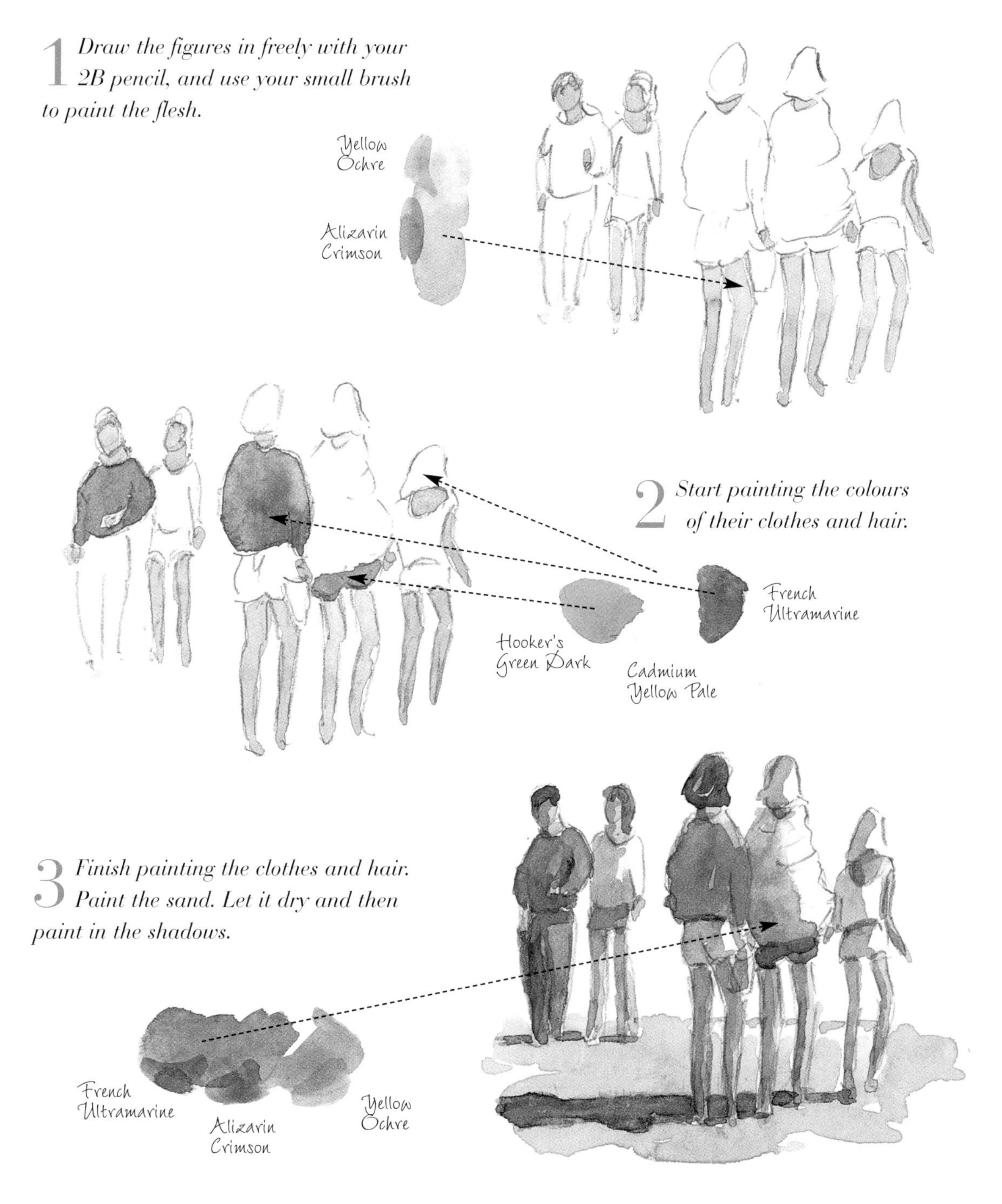

2 *Start painting the colours of their clothes and hair.*

3 *Finish painting the clothes and hair. Paint the sand. Let it dry and then paint in the shadows.*

Sketching people on the beach

Sketching people is like sketching animals and birds. They never keep still. As you can see from these sketch pages, you have to work quickly, and even then some will have gone before you get any further than a few pencil lines. Don't panic! Be patient, keep drawing and you will succeed. Start by copying my sketches, and also use photographs; this is an acceptable way to practise and it will give you confidence when you do go out to sketch.

This is as far as I got before they moved!

I was lucky this time, these figures stayed long enough.

The cast shadows from the children anchor them on the beach.

You don't need more detail than this: keep it simple.

Quick and simple, but effective.

I only had time for a very quick sketch.

Dodging the pebbles: note the legs!

Remember, shadows show sunlight.

I left the towel white to keep the picture simple.

DEMONSTRATION FAMILY GROUP

AT A GLANCE...

1 *Draw the people with your 2B pencil, taking care to try to capture their characters. The man sits very upright and sturdy, the boy is on the verge of moving, and the woman is very relaxed. Their belongings are spread out on the beach around them.*

2 *Paint the sea using your small brush. Start with blue, leaving white lines for the waves, changing to green and then to yellow for the sand. Continue painting the sand wet-on-wet. Use a directional wash around the figures, going over the boy's and woman's hair.*

The palette

French Ultramarine

Hooker's Green Dark

Cadmium Yellow Pale

Yellow Ochre

Coeruleum

Cadmium Red

Alizarin Crimson

3 *Now paint the flesh. The boy is delicate, his colours are Alizarin Crimson and Cadmium Yellow Pale with plenty of water. The man is quite suntanned; paint him using Cadmium Red and Yellow Ochre with less water. The woman is the same as the boy, with more red on her knees and cheeks.*

4 *This is the fun part, using many bright summery colours. Paint the boy's trousers, changing colours as you paint, then paint the other items in the colours as you see them. Use the rigger brush for the woman's checked shorts and the man's deck chair.*

5 *Paint the foreground sand wet-on-wet. Use a directional wash around the group's feet and belongings, adding darker and redder areas in the sand. This makes the sand more uneven than the background. It also helps to make the people and their belongings sit in the sand.*

Detail (actual size): *Notice how I haven't put detail into the face; it is too small and would look fussy. I have left the blouse as white paper which adds sparkle and simplifies the figure. Look at the difference in flesh colour between the woman and the man. She is much more delicate.*

6 ***Finished picture:*** *Bockingford watercolour paper, 18 x 23 cm (7 x 9 in). In this final stage make the people look three dimensional by adding shadows. The sun is coming from the left, so paint the shadows on the people on their right sides using your small brush. Paint darker shadows on the foreground.*

BOATS

Some artists worry that painting boats will be difficult, believing them to be too technical, and that you need to know all about them before you can draw them. But what you really need to do is to observe them very carefully, and sketch what you see. If you study a boat, you will see how it sits in the water, and where all the details go. Don't worry, your boat doesn't need to be seaworthy!

Yacht race

This was painted very quickly and freely. The dark cloudy sky and the dark water show the white sails of the yachts and their reflections up beautifully (light against dark). This is why I left the sails and some of the boats white. The effect is much more dramatic.

I painted the cloudy sky, leaving the white sails as unpainted paper. I continued into the water, changing colours on the way down, also leaving unpainted paper for the reflections. When dry, I painted the headland and boats. Note how the sails are all blowing in the same direction.

Rowing boat

This rowing boat looks relatively simple, but you will still need to study its shape to make it sit realistically either in the water, or on the sand. If you copy this one carefully it will help you when you paint one on the beach.

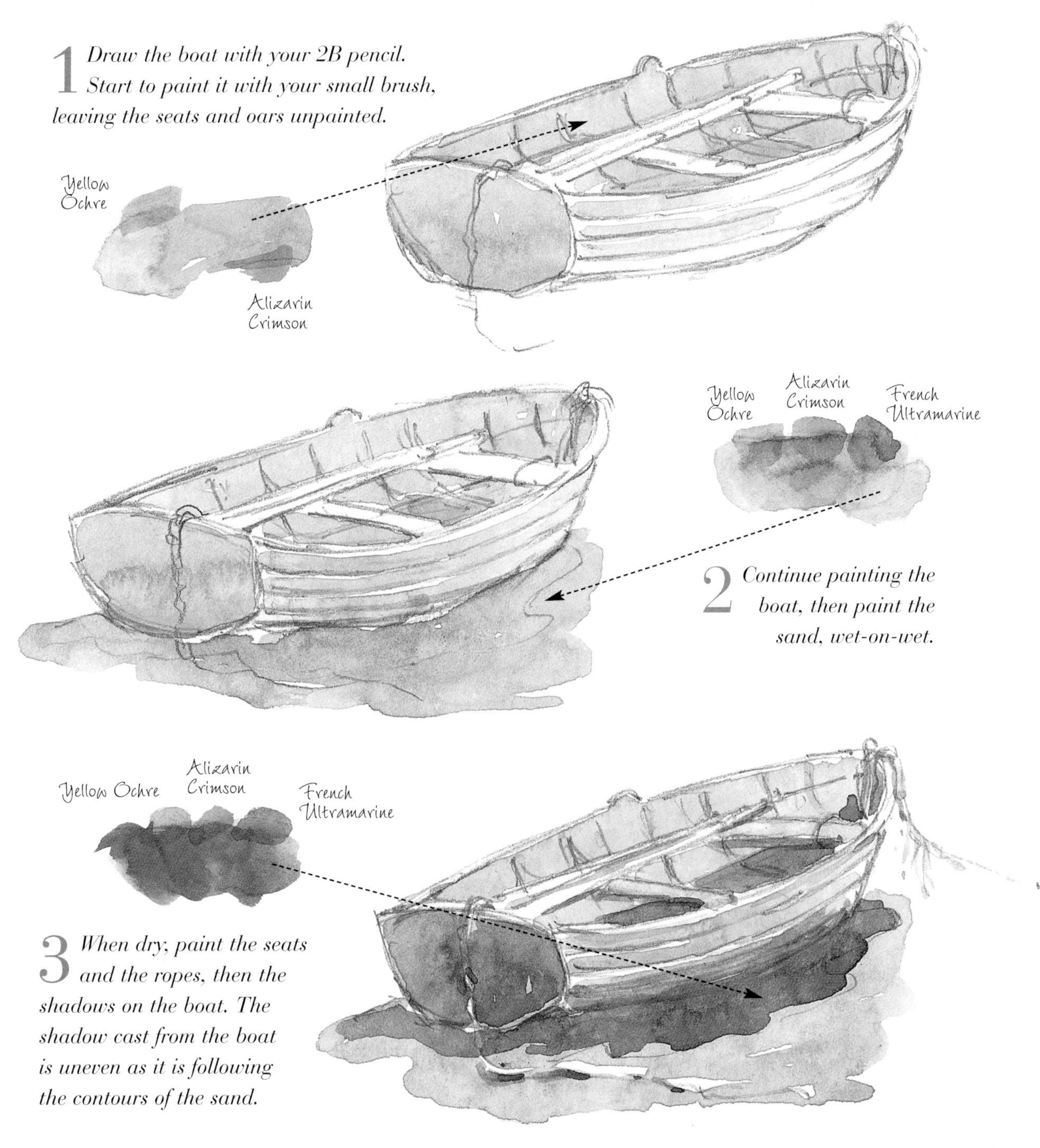

1 *Draw the boat with your 2B pencil. Start to paint it with your small brush, leaving the seats and oars unpainted.*

2 *Continue painting the boat, then paint the sand, wet-on-wet.*

3 *When dry, paint the seats and the ropes, then the shadows on the boat. The shadow cast from the boat is uneven as it is following the contours of the sand.*

Boat on the beach

Fishing boats can be very colourful, and are found in a wide variety of shapes and sizes in different areas of the world. This boat attracted me because of its character and bright red colour.

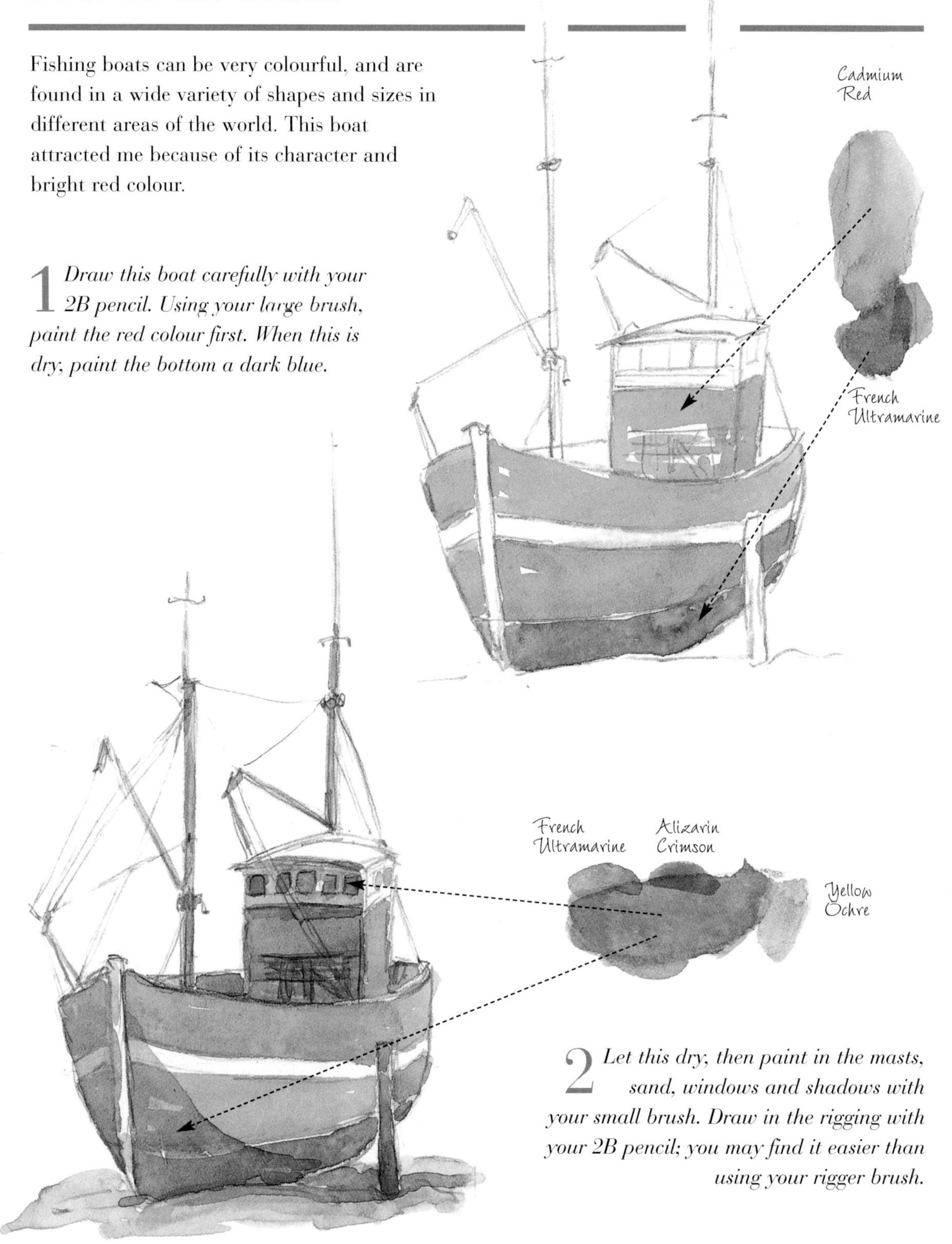

1 *Draw this boat carefully with your 2B pencil. Using your large brush, paint the red colour first. When this is dry, paint the bottom a dark blue.*

2 *Let this dry, then paint in the masts, sand, windows and shadows with your small brush. Draw in the rigging with your 2B pencil; you may find it easier than using your rigger brush.*

Thames barge

The Thames barge is a very imposing and dramatic sight, with its large brown sails and intricate rigging. It sounds rather daunting to paint, but don't forget you are painting an impression of the boat, not producing a technical drawing. I painted this the same size as it is reproduced here.

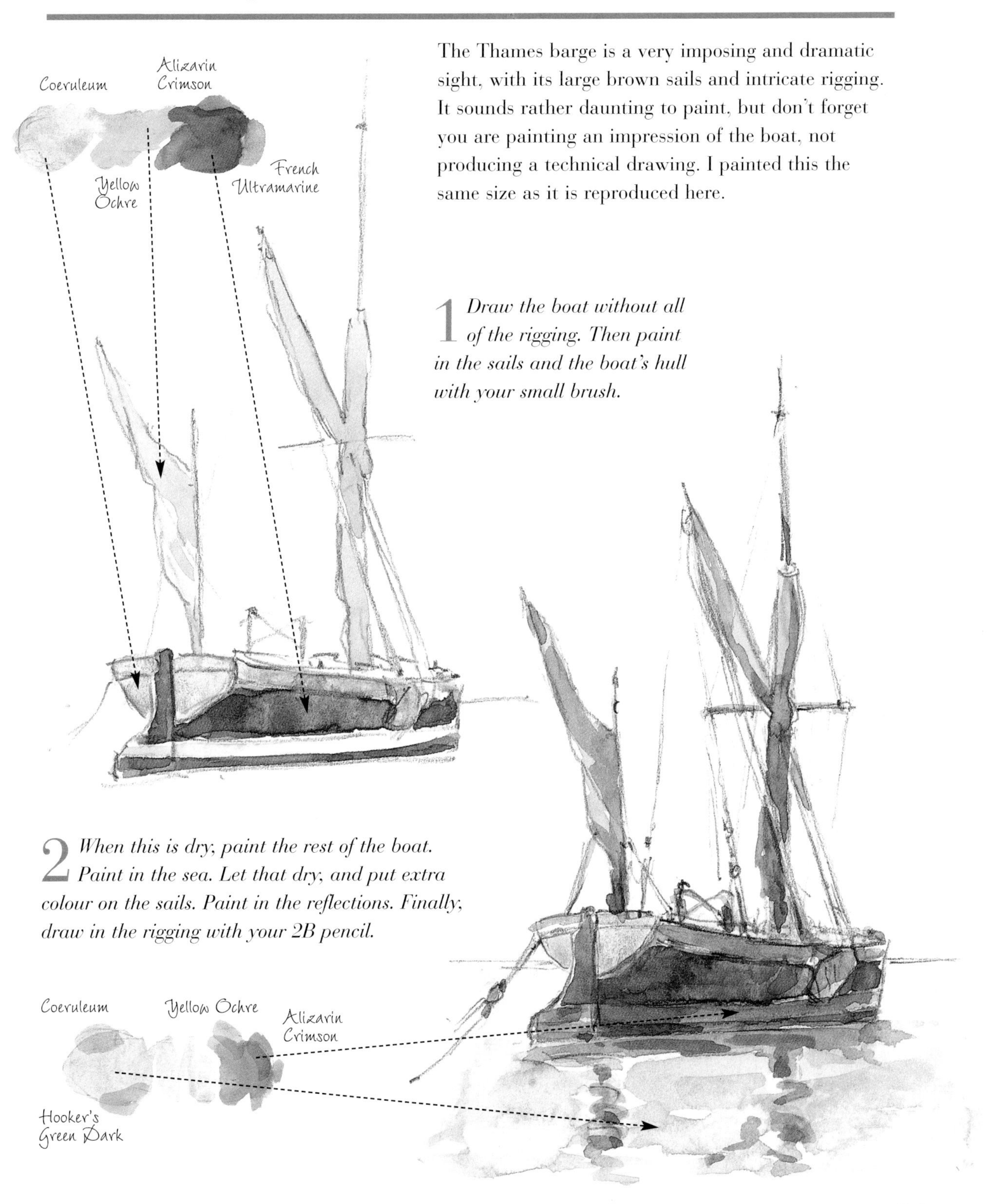

1 *Draw the boat without all of the rigging. Then paint in the sails and the boat's hull with your small brush.*

2 *When this is dry, paint the rest of the boat. Paint in the sea. Let that dry, and put extra colour on the sails. Paint in the reflections. Finally, draw in the rigging with your 2B pencil.*

Sketching boats

Sketching helps to gather information for paintings, gives you memories to keep, or can be done just for the pleasure of it. Sketches can be paintings in their own right but are not usually very detailed. If I am doing a large sketch of boats I use my rigger brush for the rigging, but if I am sketching on a small scale I sometimes use my 2B pencil.

A very windy regatta; I had to work very quickly.

Remember these sketches are very useful for information, even the silhouettes on the left.

Including a modern fibreglass boat won't spoil your painting.

I couldn't resist sketching this boat in the lovely blue-green sea.

Notice the rigging lines were left as pencil.

The shadow from this rowing boat sits it on the beach.

Here the very simple suggestion of people gives scale to the sketch.

A typical boat workshop.

DEMONSTRATION FISHING BOAT

AT A GLANCE...

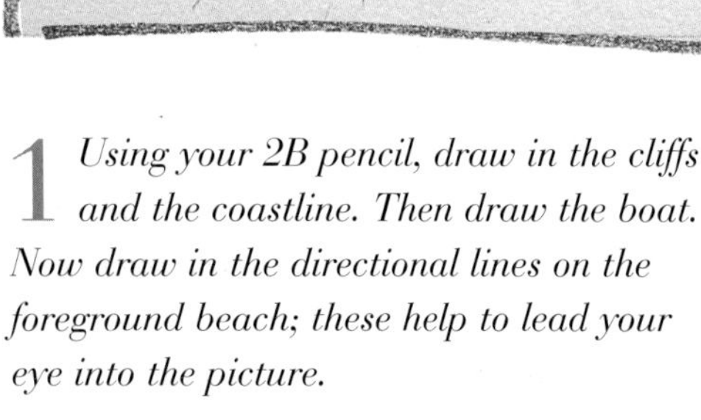

1 *Using your 2B pencil, draw in the cliffs and the coastline. Then draw the boat. Now draw in the directional lines on the foreground beach; these help to lead your eye into the picture.*

2 *Paint the sky and distant cliffs Coeruleum. When dry, paint over the distant cliffs again with pale yellow. Paint the nearer cliffs, adding red and green. Once dry, paint a shadow wash on the distant cliffs. Paint the beach.*

The palette

Coeruleum

Cadmium Yellow Pale

Yellow Ochre

French Ultramarine

Hooker's Green Dark

Alizarin Crimson

3 *Use your small brush to paint the boat with Alizarin Crimson adding Yellow Ochre where needed. Paint the blues with French Ultramarine and a touch of Alizarin Crimson, adding Hooker's Green Dark for the bottom of the boat.*

4 *Paint the sea using your small brush, wet-on-wet. Drop in red for the reflections of the fenders and a dark colour for the reflection of the boat. Next paint in the beach, leaving white lines to lead the eye into the painting.*

5 ***Finished picture:*** *Bockingford watercolour paper, 23 x 18 cm (9 x 7 in). Paint light shadows on the small rocks on the distant shore. The sun is on the right, so paint the shadows on the left side of the boat. When you paint the shadow on the bottom of the boat add more green and continue into the water. Finally, paint shadows on the beach.*